C# and XML Primer

Jonathan Hartwell

Apress®

C# and XML Primer

Jonathan Hartwell
Joliet, Illinois, USA

ISBN-13 (pbk): 978-1-4842-2594-3   ISBN-13 (electronic): 978-1-4842-2595-0
DOI 10.1007/978-1-4842-2595-0

Library of Congress Control Number: 2017933281

Managing Director: Welmoed Spahr
Editorial Director: Todd Green
Acquisitions Editor: Steve Anglin
Development Editor: Matthew Moodie
Technical Reviewer: Chaim Krause
Coordinating Editor: Mark Powers
Copy Editor: Ann Dickson
Compositor: SPi Global
Indexer: SPi Global
Artist: SPi Global
Cover image designed by Freepik

Distributed to the book trade worldwide by Springer Science+Business Media New York, 233 Spring Street, 6th Floor, New York, NY 10013. Phone 1-800-SPRINGER, fax (201) 348-4505, e-mail orders-ny@springer-sbm.com, or visit www.springeronline.com. Apress Media, LLC is a California LLC and the sole member (owner) is Springer Science + Business Media Finance Inc (SSBM Finance Inc). SSBM Finance Inc is a **Delaware** corporation.

For information on translations, please e-mail rights@apress.com, or visit http://www.apress.com/rights-permissions.

Apress titles may be purchased in bulk for academic, corporate, or promotional use. eBook versions and licenses are also available for most titles. For more information, reference our Print and eBook Bulk Sales web page at http://www.apress.com/bulk-sales.

Any source code or other supplementary material referenced by the author in this book is available to readers on GitHub via the book's product page, located at www.apress.com/9781484225943. For more detailed information, please visit http://www.apress.com/source-code.

Printed on acid-free paper

To my loving wife, Ashley, for all of the support that she has given.
And to Andy Weiss for introducing me to the world of XML with C#.

Contents at a Glance

Contents

About the Author

Jonathan Hartwell has worked professionally with C# for five years and spent four of those years handling XML. He received his master's degree in computer science from DePaul University and has an affinity for programming languages. When not programming, he is either watching Arsenal play or spending time with his wife and their two dogs. He is the founder of Voltaire Software LLC, which creates software that helps developers be more productive.

About the Technical Reviewer

Chaim Krause presently lives in Leavenworth, Kansas, where the U.S. Army employs him as a simulation specialist. In his spare time, he likes to play PC games and occasionally develops his own. He has recently taken up the sport of golf to spend more time with his significant other, Ivana. Although he holds a BA in political science from the University of Chicago, Chaim is an autodidact when it comes to computers, programming, and electronics. He wrote his first computer game in BASIC on a Tandy Model I Level I and stored the program on a cassette tape. Amateur radio introduced him to electronics while Arduino and Raspberry Pi provided a medium to combine computing, programming, and electronics into one hobby.

About the Technical Reviewer

Introduction

XML was first created in 1996 and is still in use today, both in legacy and new systems. Having been in circulation for over 20 years, there is no shortage of applications that use XML. Those applications will need to be maintained so knowledge of handling XML with C# is vital.

When you have finished this book, you are going to be able to modify, read, and write XML using C# and the .NET framework. To accommodate for legacy systems, the book discusses how to handle XML using .NET 2.0 through .NET 4.5. The book presents concepts in small pieces and then puts them together at the end in order to give a full view of how to handle XML in the real world.

The only prerequisite for this book is a basic knowledge of C#. There are extension methods that are used from LINQ but knowledge of LINQ is not required, as the classes that are needed will be covered. No knowledge of XML is assumed; however, if you do know XML, you will be able to skip a chapter.

CHAPTER 1

Introduction to XML

This chapter will cover the basics of XML and XPath. If you are already familiar with these topics, feel free to start at Chapter 2. Let's begin with a simple question that does not have such a simple answer.

What Is XML?

XML is short for *Extensible Markup Language*, which describes a document. XML consists of many parts that have no definable structure other than the structure you give to it. XML can be whatever you want or whatever somebody else wants. So let's dive into the basics. Note that this is not a comprehensive coverage of XML but gives just the basics that are needed to read, write, and modify XML.

There are two main parts to an XML document: elements and attributes. Elements, also sometimes referred to as nodes, are the backbone of XML and are what is used to describe the structure. The interesting part of elements, however, is that they can be whatever you want them to be. To demonstrate let's give an example using this book:

```
<?xml version="1.0" ?>
<book>
    <title>C# And XML: A Primer</title>
    432799_1_EnJon Hartwell</author>
</book>
```

It is quite clear as to what this data is conveying; there is a book with a title and an author. There are an opening element and closing element as well, which are necessary to have well-formed XML. All elements are going to be wrapped with < and >. The closing element will be the name of the opening element with a / before it. It is also possible to put the slash at the end of the element if there will be no children or values. That's all well and good, but what is the top line doing with the question marks? That is the XML declaration and is necessary for certain parsers to be able to identify when a document is XML.

© Jonathan Hartwell 2017
J. Hartwell, *C# and XML Primer*, DOI 10.1007/978-1-4842-2595-0_1

After elements the second most common part of XML is the attribute. The attribute goes on an element and can help describe that element. An attribute will help describe an element by giving it extra context. We could turn our book into a single element with attributes.

```
<?xml version="1.0" ?>
<book title="C# And XML: A Primer" author="Jon Hartwell" />
```

So when should you use attributes and when should you use elements? Well, that is largely up to you, but convention usually says that when you have descriptive information, it should go as an attribute. Conversely, information that is part of the data should be an element. In the above examples it makes more sense for us to put the title and author as attributes than it does as children, or elements. This is because those two pieces of information are directly tied to the book. If we were to add chapters to the example, then it would make sense for those chapters to be child elements of the book element.

XPath

XPath is a query language that was designed for parsing XML. It can be extremely useful to know XPath while working with C# and XML as many of the classes that are used in handling XML also allow the use of XPath. There are many path expressions in Xpath, but there is power in even just a few of those expressions.

The first expression that will be covered is the most basic part of XML, the element name. If you have an XML document that looks like the one below, all that would be needed to get the entire library, which is the library element, would be to use the XPath expression library. That would get not only the library element but also all descendents, or elements, below the current element. If you are already on a specific node, typically from other XPath queries, then you can use the period as the current node.

```
<library>
    <books>
        <book>
        </book>
    </books>
</library>
```

Another important element is the slash, /. This expression will get the children of the element that appears before the slash. If you want to get the books element from the above example, then you could use the slash expression and the element name of library and construct a query that looks like library/books. This query will get all elements named books that are children of library. It is important to note that the slash will only get children, which are on first level below the element, rather than descendents, which are all elements below an element.

Perhaps you just want to get a list of all the books that are in this library; that's where the double slash, //, comes in. The double slash will get all descendents of the target element. For instance, if we create a query //book, it will get the sole book that is in our XML document without having to include the library or books elements. This can be a convenience, but it can also have unintended consequences. Since this is a recursive search, if there are book elements elsewhere in the document you will pick those up too. In our library example this may not be a problem, but what about the following XML:

```
<baseballLeague>
    <team name="Tigers">
        <player name="Joe"/>
    </team>
    <team name="Saints">
        <player name="Steve"/>
    </team>
</baseballLeague>
```

If you use the XPath //player, it will give you players from both teams, which may be desirable if you are looking for all the players in the league, but it would not be what you want if you were looking for the players only on the Tigers. In general, it is best to go as deep as you can before performing a recursive search. If we wanted to get the players that are only on the Tigers, then we would have to use the attribute name as well as the elements baseballLeague and team. Remember we want to go as deep as we can before performing any filtering. From there we can filter based on the attribute name. The resulting XPath would look like baseballLeague/team[@name='Tigers'].

XSLT—Extensible Stylesheet Language

The final XML topic that we will cover is XSLT. XSLT is a bit different from XPath and straight XML as it combines both XML and XPath. An XSLT file is an XML document that transforms an XML document using XPath. Using XSLT, you can turn XML into anything you want. You could create a programming language out of XML and have XSLT turn it into C# or even machine code.

An XSLT stylesheet starts with an XML declaration and then a namespace declaration. The namespace declaration is a bit different from what we see in a traditional XML file as it is in an xsl:stylesheet element:

```
<xsl:stylesheet version="1.0"
xmlns:xsl="http://www.w3.org/1999/XSL/Transform">
```

XSLT uses templates to match XPath queries to specific XML elements within the XSLT XML file. Templates can create a pattern to match and when the pattern is seen in the XML file, it will execute the XML inside the template.

XSLT has many of the same functionalities as many programming languages such as variables, functions, if statements, and switch statements. To give an idea of what an

XSLT stylesheet looks like, we can use a mini library XML example and transform it so that it will print out the title followed by a dash and then the author:

```
<?xml version="1.0" encoding="UTF-8"?>
<library>
    <book>
        <title>The Great Gatsby</title>
        432799_1_EnF. Scott Fitzgerald</author>
    </book>
</library>
```

In order to transform the XML, we need the following stylesheet:

```
<?xml version="1.0" encoding="UTF-8"?>
<xsl:stylesheet xmlns:xsl="http://www.w3.org/1999/XSL/Transform"
xmlns="http://www.w3.org/1999/xhtml" version="1.0">
        <xsl:template match="library">
                <xsl:apply-templates />
        </xsl:template>
        <xsl:template match="book">
                <xsl:value-of select="title"/> - <xsl:value-of
                select="author"/>
        </xsl:template>
</xsl:stylesheet>
```

This small example of XSLT can be just as confusing as a larger example, so let's walk through this example. First, the XML declaration is always needed when creating an XSLT stylesheet. The declaration is followed by the the introduction of the XSL namespace. The xmlns:xsl is required; however, the other xmlns is not. There can be good reason to include extra namespaces that may not necessarily be used. In this example, we aren't using XHTML so we don't need to have that namespace included. If we were to add elements of XHTML, then that namespace would be required because it gives documentation as to what elements should be there and what structure is there. Think of it as an interface in C#. It doesn't tell you how to implement what is there, but it does tell you what has to be implemented.

To start the actual logic of the stylesheet, there needs to be a template. You can think of a template as a method in C#. The template matches on a specific element and will act on that element. You can see we have two different templates, one for library and one for book. There will always need to be a template that matches the root element of your XML file; otherwise, nothing else would be able to be run.

The final two elements of this example are the xsl:apply-templates and xsl:value-of. The element xsl:apply-templates will iterate off of the current element, in this case library, and will then try to match the correct template to that element. In our example, it will match book to the book template. In that template, you will see where we do the work that we wanted to do: write the title and author separated by a dash. We use the select attribute on the xsl:value-of to pick the element we want to output. Then if the select attribute is set to an element, it will get the child element of the current node. If it is set to an attribute, then it will get the attribute of the current node.

Wrapping Up

In this chapter, we presented an overview of XML, diving briefly into XPath and XSLT. There are more aspects in the XML family, such as Xquery, which is a programming language to query XML, as well as more in-depth topics of XPath and XSLT. If you were able to follow and understand this chapter, then you are ready to move on to the next chapter on how to read XML with C#.

CHAPTER 2

Reading XML

Reading XML is the cornerstone of handling XML in any application. If your application is unable to read XML, then you won't be able to do much. There are several ways to read XML, and this chapter will give you an insight into what methods are available to you.

Using XmlDocument

The XmlDocument class was the first way to handle reading and writing XML using the .NET Framework with C# and is included in the System.Xml namespace. With XmlDocument you can not only read XML but also manipulate and write XML, which will be covered in later chapters.

To start we will need to have an XML document to demostrate with. The following example is a small database of books and movies in our imaginary library:

Library.xml

```
<?xml version="1.0"?>
<library>
        <books>
                <book checkedout="no">
                        <title>To Kill a Mockingbird</title>
                        432799_1_EnHarper Lee</author>
                </book>
                <book checkedout="no">
                        <title>Price and Prejudice</title>
                        432799_1_EnJane Austen</author>
                </book>
                <book checkedout="yes">
                        <title>The Great Gatsby</title>
                        432799_1_EnF. Scott Fitzgerald</author>
                </book>
                <book checkedout="no">
                        <title>1984</title>
                        432799_1_EnGeorge Orwell</author>
                </book>
        </books>
```

© Jonathan Hartwell 2017
J. Hartwell, *C# and XML Primer*, DOI 10.1007/978-1-4842-2595-0_2

```
<movies>
        <movie checkedout="no">
                <title>King Kong</title>
                <year>1933</year>
        </movie>
        <movie checkedout="yes">
                <title>King Kong</title>
                <year>2005</year>
        </movie>
        <movie checkedout="yes">
                <title>To Kill A Mockingbird</title>
                <year>1962</year>
        </movie>
        <movie checkedout="no">
                <title>The Green Mile</title>
                <year>1999</year>
        </movie>
</movies>
</library>
```

To be able to do anything with this XML document, we first need to load the XML into an XmlDocument instance. There are two ways to do this: by file and by string.

Loading XML from a File

```
XmlDocument document = new XmlDocument();
document.Load("library.xml");
```

Loading XML from a String

```
XmlDocument document = new XmlDocument();
string xml = "<input>test</input>";
document.LoadXml(xml);
```

Once we have a file loaded, we can begin reading from the contents, which can be done in multiple ways.

Searching with XPath

Think of using XPath as having random read access to the XML document. It can be used to retrieve a single node or a collection of nodes. When wanting to select multiple nodes, it requires the use of the SelectNodes method. Going back to the library.xml example, we can use SelectNodes to return all the books. To get at the books, however, the proper XPath query is needed.

Starting at the top level, there is the library node, so the XPath must start with library. From there, the books child node contains all of the books that are in the library, which means that the books node is going to be appended to the XPath to give us library/books. That XPath alone will give the books node, including all of the children, but that is one step above what we want to get at so we append book to the XPath query to finally give us the query library/books/book.

```
XmlDocument document = new XmlDocument();
document.Load("library.xml");
XmlNodeList books = document.SelectNodes("library/books/book");
foreach (XmlNode book in books)
{
    richTextBox1.AppendText(book.OuterXml + Environment.NewLine);
}
```

The above code creates an instance of the XmlDocument and loads the library.xml file into XmlDocument instance, document. Once the XML is loaded into the document, SelectNodes is used since we are looking for multiple book nodes instead of a specific one. If there was only one book node in the document, then it would return the single element in the XmlNodeList. The property OuterXml is used to get the XML of the current node. There are other properties that get various XML elements from an XmlNode, which will be covered later in this chapter. This example is writing to a RichTextBox that is in a Windows form application, which is included in the downloadable source and gives us the XML content of each book printed on a new line, as shown in Figure 2-1.

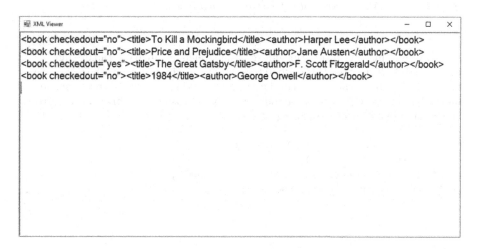

Figure 2-1. *Output from XML Viewer application based on the code above*

With the code above, you can modify the XPath query to get an XML list of any of the nodes. For instance, if we want to get a list of the movies that are available, then we modify the XPath to library/movies/movie. That would give us the following (see Figure 2-2):

```
XmlDocument document = new XmlDocument();
document.Load("library.xml");
XmlNodeList movies = document.SelectNodes("library/movies/movie");
foreach (XmlNode movie in movies)
```

```
{
        richTextBox1.AppendText(movie.OuterXml +        Environment.NewLine);
}
```

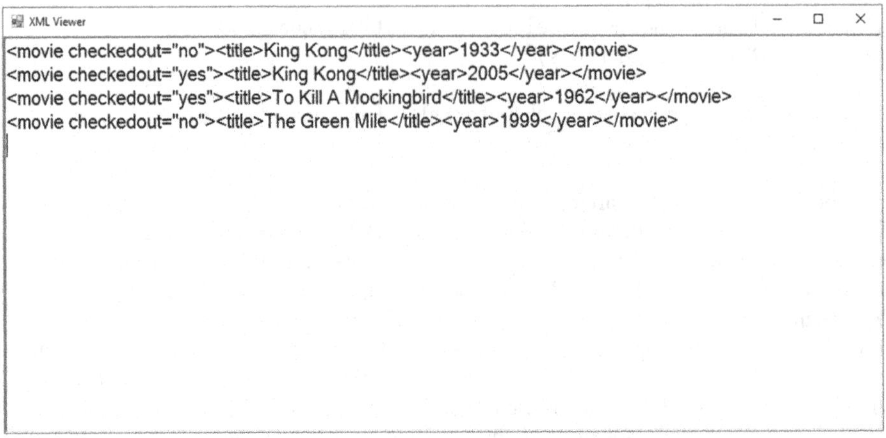

Figure 2-2. The XML Viewer results of selecting all movie nodes

If you know that you are only looking for a single element, then you can use the SelectSingleNode method. This method takes an XPath expression and returns a single XmlNode. This method will always return a single node as long as a node is returned, no matter what the query. If we have the code below execute using our library.xml file, we will get a single book that looks like Figure 2-3.

```
XmlDocument document = new XmlDocument();
document.Load("library.xml");
XmlNode book = document.SelectSingleNode("//book");
richTextBox1.AppendText(book.InnerXml);
```

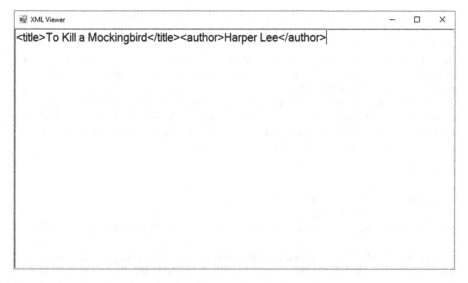

Figure 2-3. *Single book output produced by SelectSingleNode*

You'll notice that the output above returns the first book that is under the books element. SelectSingleNode will take whatever element it sees first and return that for the given XPath expression. There are ways to get a specific node though using a query such as the following:

```
XmlNode book = document.SelectSingleNode("/library/books/book[title = 'The
Great Gatsby']");
```

The query will return the same book element that we saw above, but in this example it is using a filter to find the book that has the title *To Kill a Mockingbird*.

Search Using Attributes

Up until now, there has been a focus solely on searching based on elements. There is more that can be searched on than just elements. For instance, let's say somebody asks us to find all books that are checked out. It is an easy feat if we just use SelectNodes with XPath.

Explicitly Finding Movies and Books That Are Not Checked Out

```
XmlDocument document = new XmlDocument();
document.Load("library.xml");
XmlNodeList movies = document.SelectNodes("library/books/book[@
checkedout='yes'] | library/movies/movie[@checkedout='no']");
```

The above code uses the attribute notation to find both movies and books that are not checked out. In order to search for both, it is necessary to add a pipe between the two XPath queries. You can think of it like the double pipe OR statement in C#. This notation is useful when there are many different children of the root element and you want to filter it down. If we had CDs in this library, we would be able to use the above code to only find books and movies and ignore the CDs.

The problem with the above code is that it is very verbose, especially if there are many children of the node that you are searching under. There is an easier way to find this information without having to type out every single possibility and that is to use the star operator and recursive search in XPath.

Using the Recursive Search and Star

```
XmlDocument document = new XmlDocument();
document.Load("library.xml");
XmlNodeList movies = document.SelectNodes("library//*[@checkedout='no']");
```

The above code contains two different shortcuts. First, there is the double slash. This is a way to get all children recursively. For this library XML file, this means it would look not only at the books and movies elements but also the children of those nodes. This gives us access to all elements under the library node. Be careful when using the double slash in your XPath queries as it will select **all** elements regardless of the type of element. If any other elements were added to the library element, those elements would be included in the results as well.

The second shortcut that is in the code above is the star. The star is a shortcut that ignores the element type. What that means is that it treats an element of book the same as the movie element. It is extremely useful when you have several different children or grandchildren under a single element and want to search all of them. We don't have to use the | operator to combine multiple queries, which drastically cuts down on the amount of code that is needed.

The previous example used attributes to search, but it is also possible to inspect what attributes are on an element by using the Attributes property. Attributes will return an XmlAttributeCollection, which can be iterated on.

```
XmlDocument doc = new XmlDocument();
doc.Load("library.xml");
XmlNodeList books = doc.SelectNodes("//book");
foreach(XmlNode book in books)
{
    var attributes = book.Attributes;
    foreach(XmlAttribute attr in attributes)
    {
        richTextBox1.AppendText(attr.Value + Environment.NewLine);
    }
}
```

In the code above, there is the standard iteration that has been seen when dealing with XmlNodes in the past but, alas, there is one difference: the use of Value. Attributes do not have InnerText or InnerXml values. When trying to get an attribute's text, you will be scratching your head wondering why the attribute you know has a value isn't showing any value. When using the Value attribute, the only text that will show is the text that is surrounded by the quotes for that attribute. When running the code above, you will get the output in Figure 2-4.

Figure 2-4. *The checkedout attribute for all of the books in the library*

Handling Namespaces

Up until now, there only has been straight XML with no namespaces required. While this may happen when you have full control of the XML, chances are that you will encounter namespaces and will need to know how to handle them when it comes to using the XmlDocument class. Namespaces are useful when it comes to preventing collisions with names and so the XmlDocument must take that into consideration.

```
<?xml version="1.0"?>
<library xmlns:network="www.library.com">
      <books>
              <book checkedout="no">
                      <title>To Kill a Mockingbird</title>
                      <author>Harper Lee</author>
              </book>
              <book checkedout="no">
                      <title>Price and Prejudice</title>
                      <author>Jane Austen</author>
              </book>
```

13

```
            <book checkedout="yes">
                    <title>The Great Gatsby</title>
                    <author>F. Scott Fitzgerald</author>
            </book>
            <book checkedout="no">
                    <title>1984</title>
                    <author>George Orwell</author>
            </book>
    </books>
    <movies>
            <movie checkedout="no">
                    <title>King Kong</title>
                    <year>1933</year>
            </movie>
            <movie checkedout="yes">
                    <title>King Kong</title>
                    <year>2005</year>
            </movie>
            <movie checkedout="yes">
                    <title>To Kill A Mockingbird</title>
                    <year>1962</year>
            </movie>
            <movie checkedout="no">
                    <title>The Green Mile</title>
                    <year>1999</year>
            </movie>
    </movies>
</library>
```

As we have added a new namespace to our library.xml example, we need to load the namespace into our XmlDocument:

Adding a Namespace to the XmlDocument before Loading XML

```
XmlDocument document = new XmlDocument();
XmlNamespaceManager namespaceManager = new XmlNamespaceManager(document.
NameTable);
namespaceManager.AddNamespace("network", "http://www.library.com");
document.Load("library-network.xml");
```

In order to add a namespace to an XmlDocument, it is necessary to use the name table, which is of type XmlNameTable, from the XmlDocument. This is the class that handles keeping track of all of the namespaces. Once we have that, an XmlNamespaceManager needs to be created as that is what will allow us to add or remove namespaces. Being able to remove a namespace is just using the RemoveNamespace method of XmlNamespaceManager, which takes the same arguments as AddNamespace.

Using XPathDocument

The XPathDocument class is similar to the XmlDocument class, but the difference is that, unlike XmlDocument, XPathDocument is read only. It is excellent for reading XML when you have no intention of modifying the data. The XPathDocument class relies on two separate classes to do the actual querying: XPathNavigator and XPathNodeIterator.

The XPathNavigator class is what is used to actually query the XML. It allows the use of XPath queries or generic methods that allow you to get at elements and attributes without having to know any XPath.

In order to start using the XPathNavigator, there are two steps involved. An XPathDocument needs to be instantiated and then use that instance to create the XPathNavigator. Once the XPathNavigator is instantiated, it will open up the ability to query the XML.

Create XPathDocument and XPathNavigator Instances

```
XPathDocument xPathDocument = new XPathDocument("library.xml");
XPathNavigator navigator = xPathDocument.CreateNavigator();
```

The XPathNavigator is only the first step into being able to read and query XML. To query the document, one must create an XPathNodeIterator. The XPathNodeIterator will provide access to all the elements under the root element.

Iterating on the Children of the Root Element

```
XPathDocument xpathDocument = new XPathDocument("library.xml");
XPathNavigator navigator = xpathDocument.CreateNavigator();
XPathNodeIterator iterator = navigator.SelectChildren(XPathNodeType.
Element);

while (iterator.MoveNext())
{
    richTextBox1.AppendText(iterator.Current.Value);
}
```

Reading with XmlReader

XmlReader is different from the other XML handling classes that we have used as it is stream-based. What that means for us is that it will only operate going forward and prevents querying. XmlReader is a good option if you are handling large XML files and don't care about random access to the elements in the XML document. Because XmlReader uses streams to load the XML document, you can read in files that are too large for the XmlDocument. XmlReaders require much more setup than the other classes we've looked at prior, but because of their ability to handle large data it is more than worth it. We can start with a basic example:

Creating an XmlReader and Reading the Library File

```
StreamReader xmlStream = new StreamReader("library.xml");
using (XmlReader reader = XmlReader.Create(xmlStream))
{
    while(reader.Read())
    {
        richTextBox1.AppendText(reader.Value + Environment.NewLine);
    }
}
```

The output of this will present a quite different view from what we have seen already (Figure 2-5).

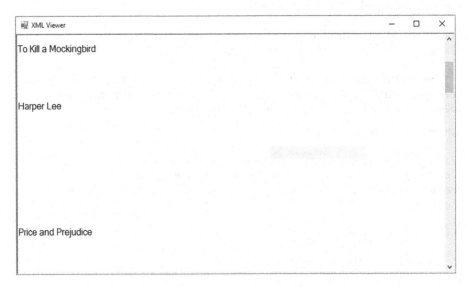

Figure 2-5. *The values of the XML elements from the library.xml that has gone through the XmlReader*

Notice that there is a lot of blank space as well as only the values. The reason for that is the way that the XmlReader handles the underlying XML stream. Remember it is a forward-only stream. Since we used the value property, it is only going to give us the values of elements that have one. But why the space? Simple. Each one of those spaces represents an element that did not have a value. This is where XmlReader becomes more complicated than other methods of reading; it doesn't differentiate the type of XML that is being read. The reader does store the type information, but we must manually check it. If we want to get at the type, we can use the XmlNodeType enumeration. We have only been focusing on elements and attributes, so let's create a reader that will handle both.

Handling Both Elements and Values

```
StreamReader xmlStream = new StreamReader("library.xml");
using (XmlReader reader = XmlReader.Create(xmlStream))
{
    while(reader.Read())
    {
        switch (reader.NodeType)
        {
            case XmlNodeType.Element:
                richTextBox1.AppendText(reader.Name + Environment.NewLine);
                break;
            case XmlNodeType.Text:
                richTextBox1.AppendText(reader.Value + Environment.NewLine);
                break;
            case XmlNodeType.EndElement:
                richTextBox1.AppendText(reader.Name + Environment.NewLine);
                    break;
            default:
                break;
        }
    }
}
```

The element node type is added as well as the EndElement node type. There is a good reason that you may want to include both. If you just include element, you will get the element name and then the value of that element followed by the next element. On the other hand, if you include both EndElement and element, it will give you Figure 2-6.

Figure 2-6. Output of the XmlReader once we put checks in for specific type being read

Remember when I said there was a reason you would want both? That reason is when you want to write the XML, you are reading from the XmlReader stream.

Using LINQ to XML

XmlDocument was introduced in .NET 2.0 and remained the only way to handle XML until .NET 3.5 was released. In the .NET 3.5 release, we saw the introduction of LINQ (Language Integrated Query) and the advent of LINQ to XML. LINQ to XML is now the preferred method of handling XML, so let's dive in using the library XML example from the last section.

XDocument is LINQ to XML's equivelent to the XmlDocument. The nature of LINQ gives XDocument a whole different feel, but don't worry because you can still fall back on XPath. For instance, the following code will instantiate an XDocument as well as get the values of every book.

```
XDocument doc = new XDocument();
doc = XDocument.Load("library.xml");
IEnumerable<XElement> books = doc.Descendants().Where(x => x.Name ==
"book");
foreach(XElement book in books)
{
    richTextBox1.AppendText(book.Value + Environment.NewLine);
}
```

This approach gives a much cleaner interface, and it is clear on what is happening to those who aren't well versed in XPath. That being said, the Value property of the XElement book is not as clear as one might think. Instead of giving XML, it returns all children and concatenates the values of those children, as seen in Figure 2-7.

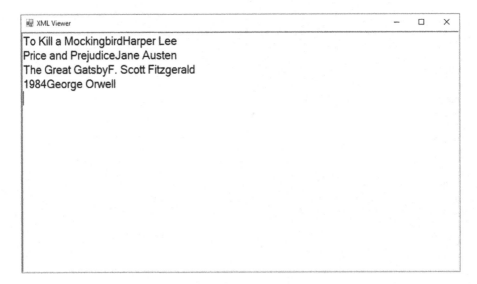

Figure 2-7. Output from the LINQ to XML query

Document vs. Document.Root: Getting to the Root Document

There are two ways to get at the root element using XDocument: using the instantiated XDocument class directly or using the Root property on the instantiated class. There is a subtle difference and that is the Root property is an XElement instead of an XDocument. Because of that, you are able to use all of the methods that you would normally get with XElement but by using the root element directly.

We used the XDocument in the example above because the XDocument allows access to the descendants of the root element, which is what we needed in order to traverse the XML structure and find the book elements. If we had used the Root property, it would have allowed us to not only get descendants but to add elements as well as get to the attributes of the root element.

Searching for Attributes

We saw how to search using attributes when handling XML with XmlDocument and how it required XPath to get at the attributes relatively easily; that same task becomes much easier with XML to LINQ. Let's say we want to find all the elements that have a checkedout attribute. We can use our LINQ expressions to find all elements that have the checkedout attribute.

```
List<XElement> elementsWithAttributes = document.Descendants().Where(x =>
x.HasAttributes && x.Attribute("checkedout") != null).ToList();
```

There is a drawback to using LINQ, which is that it is much more verbose than using straight XPath. With XDocument we could still use XPath to get the same results. Where LINQ shines is when you have more complex queries that may be difficult to read in XPath or require more in-depth knowledge of XPath. For instance, we could look for all movie and book elements, which we did in the previous chapter by using LINQ instead of XPath.

```
List<XElement> booksOrMovies = document.Descendants().Where(x => x.Name ==
"movie" || x.Name == "book").ToList();
```

Or we could retrieve movies that were released between certain years. For instance, let's look for movies that were released between 1990 and 2016. That would be an incredibly complex XPath query that would be horrible to maintain in the future. On the other hand, by using LINQ and XDocument it becomes a simple where clause to filter out the unwanted titles. We can do all that in the following code:

```
List<XElement> movies = document.Descendants()
    .Where(x => x.Name == "year" && (int.Parse(x.Value) >= 1990 && int.
Parse(x.Value) <= 2015))
    .Select(x => x.Parent).ToList();
```

Now there are many things in the above code that may need an explanation because we have not seen it before or it may not be intuitive. First off, we are searching for the year element instead of directly for a movie element. This allows us to easily get at the value of that element, which is the year the movie was made, instead of having to filter down even more based on the movie element's children. The only reason why that method is feasible is because of the Parent property. The Parent property will return the XElement of the parent of the current XElement. In this case, the element movie is the parent of the title element, so we can get back up to the movie element after we are done filtering. We are also doing some parsing of the year into integer type; however, this is not recommended in production code as this could throw exceptions. I am doing this here for demonstration purposes.

Transforming Results

LINQ to XML allows us to use all of the extension methods that come with LINQ, which gives us access to the Select method. This method can allow us to transform our results into a different class or anonymous class. We have a way to get to the books in our XML library, but we haven't done anything with them yet. That is about to change. We are going to capture the information about the books and put them in a C# class called Book that is defined below.

```
class Book
{
    public string Author { get; set; }
    public string Title { get; set; }
}
List<Book> books = document.Descendants()
    .Where(x => x.Name == "book")
    .Select(x => new Book()
        { Title = x.Element("title").Value,
          Author = x.Element("author").Value
        }).ToList();
```

The above code filters the XML document down to just book elements and then transforms the title and author into a new Book class that we had defined. Notice that the Element method is used instead of Descendants because we know that the title and author elements are children of the book element, rather than grandchildren, so we don't need to go any deeper.

Using XPath with XDocument

As mentioned before, it is possible to use XPath with XDocument, though not recommended. For instance, we could use XPath to get a list of all movies:

```
List<XElement> movies = document.XPathSelectElements("//movie").ToList();
```

One thing to note is that this does not return XmlNode like the XmlDocument does, but instead returns XElement. There is also the XPathSelectElement method, which is equivalent to the XmlDocument SelectSingleNode. Just like SelectSingleNode, if you use an XPath query that will return multiple results, the first element is only returned.

```
XElement movie = document.XPathSelectElement("//movie");
```

In the end, LINQ to XML allows for easy access to querying data from an XML document in a more consistent format as well.

CHAPTER 3

■ ■ ■

Modifying XML

Reading XML is only one part of handling XML in C#. Once you have an XML document loaded, there are times you need to make modifications, especially if you plan to write the XML back to file. The following steps take you through the process of modifying XML with both XmlDocument as well as XDocument. We will continue to use the library XML in this chapter and will also assume that all the XML has been loaded into an instantiated XmlDocument or XDocument named document. As a reminder, following is the library XML:

```xml
<?xml version="1.0"?>
<library>
    <books>
        <book checkedout="no">
            <title>To Kill a Mockingbird</title>
            <author>Harper Lee</author>
        </book>
        <book checkedout="no">
            <title>Price and Prejudice</title>
            <author>Jane Austen</author>
        </book>
        <book checkedout="yes">
            <title>The Great Gatsby</title>
            <author>F. Scott Fitzgerald</author>
        </book>
        <book checkedout="no">
            <title>1984</title>
            <author>George Orwell</author>
        </book>
    </books>
    <movies>
        <movie checkedout="no">
            <title>King Kong</title>
            <year>1933</year>
        </movie>
        <movie checkedout="yes">
            <title>King Kong</title>
            <year>2005</year>
```

© Jonathan Hartwell 2017

J. Hartwell, *C# and XML Primer*, DOI 10.1007/978-1-4842-2595-0_3

```
        </movie>
        <movie checkedout="yes">
                <title>To Kill A Mockingbird</title>
                <year>1962</year>
        </movie>
        <movie checkedout="no">
                <title>The Green Mile</title>
                <year>1999</year>
        </movie>
    </movies>
</library>
```

Using XmlDocument

Let's start with XmlDocument.

Modifying Attributes

Since we are using a library as an example, then the most common modification would be to check out or check in a book. Since the library XML structure is using checked in or checked out as an attribute, we must learn how to modify attributes to ensure the library has a proper listing of books. To start, though, we need to ensure we have the right book. For this example, a patron of the library is checking out *To Kill a Mockingbird*. First, we need to find the book and then we can modify the attribute. Modifying the attribute is no different that just setting a value in a dictionary. After all, that is all that the Attributes property on XmlNode truly is.

```
XmlDocument doc = new XmlDocument();
doc.Load("library.xml");
XmlNode book = doc.SelectSingleNode("//book[title='To Kill a
Mockingbird']");
book.Attributes["checkedout"].Value = "yes";
```

The above code will change our attribute from "no" to "yes", as you can see in Figure 3-1.

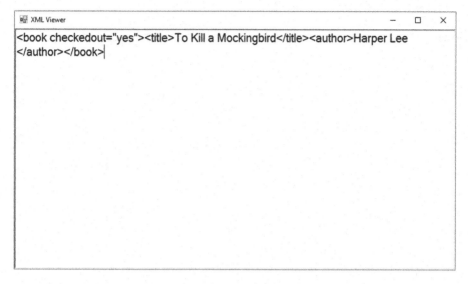

Figure 3-1. *Book XML after modifying the checkedout attribute*

Modifying Elements

We have already changed the attribute of a book showing that a book has been checked out, so let's take it a step further and change an element. Let's say we have a new edition of a movie that is released in a different year than what we already have. We will need to change that year element so that it will properly reflect what is currently in the library. In this example, we will say that there was a ten-year anniversary release of the *Green Mile* that the library bought. Because of that, we will need to update the year on that specific movie.

```
XmlDocument doc = new XmlDocument();
doc.Load("library.xml");
XmlNode movie = doc.SelectSingleNode("//movie[title='The Green Mile']");
XmlNode movieYear = movie.SelectSingleNode("year");
movieYear.InnerText = "2009";
```

We first select the movie node and then get the year element under that movie node. Once we have that element, we are free to change the value. Notice that we must use the InnerText property instead of Value. It is one of the many inconsistencies that arise when dealing with XmlDocument and its related classes. If you end up writing code that has an element that should have a value but doesn't, check to see if you are using Value instead of InnerText. When you run the above code, it will give you the output in Figure 3-2.

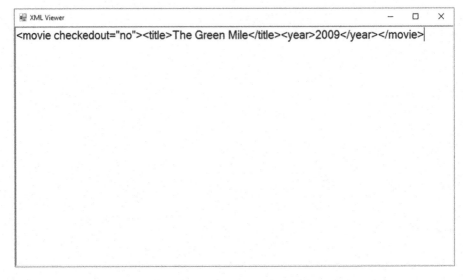

Figure 3-2. The Green Mile tenth-anniversary update to the library

Adding Attributes

In a library people may accidentally damage a movie, especially if it is a DVD and easily scratchable. Currently our library doesn't track that kind of damage, so let's add the ability to track it as an attribute. After all, this is a descriptive feature of the movie.

```
XmlDocument doc = new XmlDocument();
doc.Load("library.xml");
XmlNodeList movies = doc.SelectNodes("//movie");
foreach(XmlNode movie in movies)
{
    XmlAttribute attribute = doc.CreateAttribute("damaged");
    attribute.Value = "no";
    movie.Attributes.Append(attribute);
}
```

Now the code that was used to create an attribute is not as straightforward as one would expect. After all, we were accessing an attribute just like it was part of a dictionary. In order to create an attribute, we must use the instance of the XmlDocument class that will be using the attribute. In other words, if you are going to put the attribute on XML in the document represented by an instance of XmlDocument, then you need to use that instance to create the attribute via the CreateAttribute method. Now that we have an instance of XmlAttribute, we can modify the value and then add to the instance of the XmlNode movie. Figure 3-3 displays what the movie elements look like after the addition of the attribute.

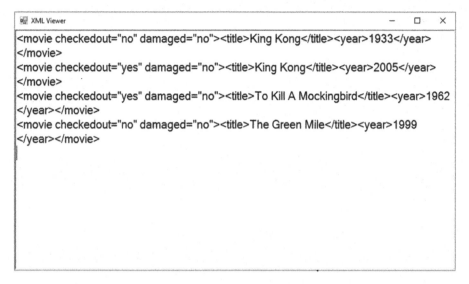

Figure 3-3. *The output after adding the damaged attribute*

Adding Elements

We have added a damaged attribute to the movie elements in our library, but that isn't all we have to do. A library will always get more items in its collection, so we should discuss how to do that. Let's say that our library has bought a new book for its collection. We can create that book in a similar way to creating the attributes previously.

```
XmlDocument doc = new XmlDocument();
doc.Load("library.xml");
XmlNode book = doc.CreateElement("book");
XmlAttribute checkedOut = doc.CreateAttribute("checkedout");
XmlAttribute damaged = doc.CreateAttribute("damaged");
checkedOut.Value = "no";
damaged.Value = "no";
book.Attributes.Append(checkedOut);
book.Attributes.Append(damaged);
```

In the code above we see that the CreateElement method is called from the instance of XmlDocument. This creates an XmlNode that has the name "book". Once we have our book element, we will need to add the attributes using the same technique we did earlier. The output from this code is shown in Figure 3-4.

27

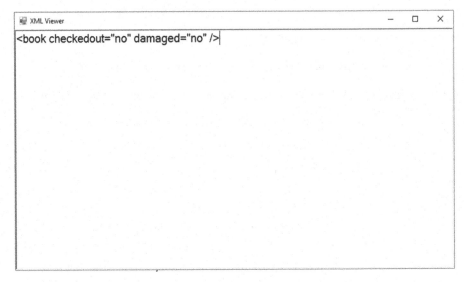

Figure 3-4. *The output from creating a new book element*

We have a book element, but we don't have all of the information for this book. We are missing a title and author, so let's add that now, but first we need to create the new elements.

```
XmlNode title = doc.CreateElement("title");
title.InnerText = "A Clockwork Orange";
XmlNode year = doc.CreateElement("year");
year.InnerText = "1962";
book.AppendChild(title);
book.AppendChild(year);
```

Using the instance of XmlDocument, "doc", and XmlNode, "book", from above, we can create the new instances of XmlNodes by using the CreateElement method, just as we have done before. The new method comes in the form of AppendChild. The AppendChild method will take an XmlNode and add it as child of the XmlNode instance that is calling the method. Note that the elements will be placed in the order that they added in the resulting XML output. The full code example is below with the output shown in Figure 3-5:

```
XmlDocument doc = new XmlDocument();
doc.Load("library.xml");

XmlNode book = doc.CreateElement("book");
XmlAttribute checkedOut = doc.CreateAttribute("checkedout");
XmlAttribute damaged = doc.CreateAttribute("damaged");
checkedOut.Value = "no";
damaged.Value = "no";
book.Attributes.Append(checkedOut);
book.Attributes.Append(damaged);
```

28

```
XmlNode title = doc.CreateElement("title");
title.InnerText = "A Clockwork Orange";
XmlNode year = doc.CreateElement("year");
year.InnerText = "1962";
book.AppendChild(title);
book.AppendChild(year);
```

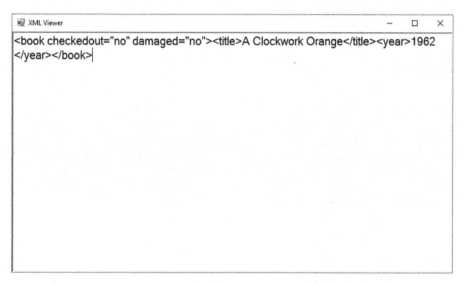

Figure 3-5. *The output from adding the attributes as well as children to the book*

We have one final step before we can say we have added a new book to our library and that is actually adding it back to the underlying XML library. To do this, we need to get an instance of the books element and then we can just use the AppendChild method on that instance to add the book. If we use the book instance from prior code example, you can see we just need to add two more lines:

```
XmlNode books = doc.SelectSingleNode("//books");
books.AppendChild(book);
```

The full code example is below as well as the output in Figure 3-6:

```
XmlDocument doc = new XmlDocument();
doc.Load("library.xml");

XmlNode book = doc.CreateElement("book");
XmlAttribute checkedOut = doc.CreateAttribute("checkedout");
XmlAttribute damaged = doc.CreateAttribute("damaged");
checkedOut.Value = "no";
damaged.Value = "no";
```

29

```
book.Attributes.Append(checkedOut);
book.Attributes.Append(damaged);

XmlNode title = doc.CreateElement("title");
title.InnerText = "A Clockwork Orange";
XmlNode year = doc.CreateElement("year");
year.InnerText = "1962";
book.AppendChild(title);
book.AppendChild(year);

XmlNode books = doc.SelectSingleNode("//books");
books.AppendChild(book);
```

![XML Viewer] XML Viewer	— ☐ ✕
`<books><book checkedout="no"><title>To Kill a Mockingbird</title><author>Harper Lee</author></book><book checkedout="no"><title>Price and Prejudice</title><author>Jane Austen</author></book><book checkedout="yes"><title>The Great Gatsby</title><author>F. Scott Fitzgerald</author></book><book checkedout="no"><title>1984</title><author>George Orwell</author></book><book checkedout="no" damaged="no"><title>A Clockwork Orange</title><year>1962</year></book></books>`	

Figure 3-6. *The final output of the books element after adding A Clockwork Orange to our library*

Merging Documents

Let's say that you have two XML documents that now need to be merged into one single XML document. You could do it by hand or you could use C# and XmlDocument in order to merge them.

Merging two or more XmlDocuments is not as straightforward as selecting a single element and then adding it to the other XmlDocument. The XmlDocument only allows an XmlNode to exist in one document, which is why you aren't able to do a straight copy since the reference to the source document still exists. Instead, you must import the node into the new document by using ImportNode method. This can allow adding deep, which means adding this specific XmlNode and all of its children, or shallow, which would only add the XmlNode with no children. In the code below, we load the library two times and then take the first movie from the source library and add it to the target library. You could think of this as two different libraries that are in a network together where one movie is checked out in the first library and returned in the second. (See Figure 3-7.)

```
XmlDocument source = new XmlDocument();
source.Load("library.xml");
XmlDocument target = new XmlDocument();
target.Load("library.xml");
XmlNodeList movies = source.SelectNodes("//movie");
XmlNode movie = target.ImportNode(movies[0], true);
target.SelectSingleNode("//movies").AppendChild(movie);
```

XML Viewer   —   □   ✕

```
<?xml version="1.0"?><library xmlns:network="www.library.com"><books><book
checkedout="no"><title>To Kill a Mockingbird</title><author>Harper Lee</author>
</book><book checkedout="no"><title>Price and Prejudice</title><author>Jane Austen
</author></book><book checkedout="yes"><title>The Great Gatsby</title><author>F.
Scott Fitzgerald</author></book><book checkedout="no"><title>1984</title><author>
George Orwell</author></book></books><movies><movie checkedout="no"><title>King
Kong</title><year>1933</year></movie><movie checkedout="yes"><title>King Kong
</title><year>2005</year></movie><movie checkedout="yes"><title>To Kill A
Mockingbird</title><year>1962</year></movie><movie checkedout="no"><title>The
Green Mile</title><year>1999</year></movie><movie checkedout="no"><title>King
Kong</title><year>1933</year></movie></movies></library>|
```

Figure 3-7. InnerXML output from the movies element

Notice that in Figure 3-7 the movie *King Kong* is present three times. The first two are expected, but then the last *King Kong* at the bottom of the movies element is a duplicate of the first *King Kong*. That is the element we added from the source.

The previous example copied using a deep copy, but what if we don't want to bring in all child elements? We can use the ImportNode method again, but this time pass in a false for the deep copy argument instead of true. This time let's select all the movies by using XPath to query on the movies element and then move the movies element, with no children, over to the target document. (See Figure 3-8.)

```
XmlDocument source = new XmlDocument();
source.Load("library.xml");
XmlDocument target = new XmlDocument();
target.Load("library.xml");
XmlNode movie = source.SelectSingleNode("//movies");
XmlNode targetMovie = target.ImportNode(movie, false);
target.SelectSingleNode("library").AppendChild(targetMovie);
```

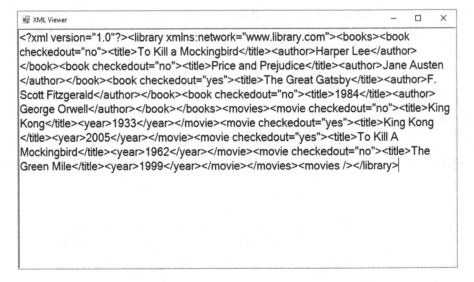

Figure 3-8. *Library version after merging two libraries*

From the output in Figure 3-8, you can see that an empty movies element was added to the library. There was just a small code change, changing true to false, and it drastically altered the way that the XML is copied.

Removing Attributes

Let's say that our library is getting rid of *Pride and Prejudice* and pulling it out of circulation. The first thing that would need to be done is to remove the ability for the book to be checked out. In order for that to happen, though, we need to remove the checkedout attribute.

When removing an attribute, we need to get the XmlNode instance that contains the attribute. In this case, we use XPath to get the book element. From there we can get to the attributes by using the Attributes property on the XmlNode, prideAndPrejudice. After that, we get the checkedout attribute from the Attributes property. Once we have the instance of the XmlAttribute checkedout, we can then go ahead and remove it by using the Remove method from the Attributes property. The output from this can be seen in Figure 3-9.

```
XmlDocument doc = new XmlDocument();
doc.Load("library.xml");
XmlNode prideAndPrejudice = doc.SelectSingleNode("//book[title='Price and
Prejudice']");
XmlAttribute checkedOut = prideAndPrejudice.Attributes["checkedout"];
prideAndPrejudice.Attributes.Remove(checkedOut);
```

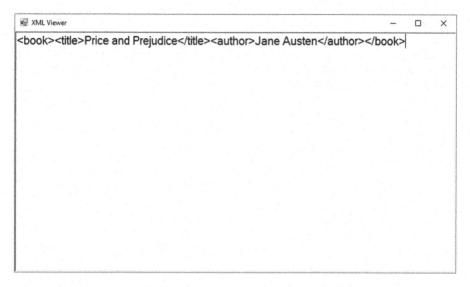

Figure 3-9. *The output of Pride and Prejudice book after removing the checkedout attribute*

Removing Elements

After removing the attributes from *Pride and Prejudice*, we want to remove the book entirely. In order to do that, we must remove the XmlNode instance that represents this book.

```
XmlDocument doc = new XmlDocument();
doc.Load("library.xml");
XmlNode books = doc.SelectSingleNode("//books");
XmlNode prideAndPrejudice = books.SelectSingleNode("//book[title='Price and
Prejudice']");
books.RemoveChild(prideAndPrejudice);
```

We first have to get the parent node of the element we want to remove. This is because the method to remove an XmlNode will only remove children and not any descendent that is further than a child. Once we have the books instance of XmlNode, we then need to search for our *Pride and Prejudice* book XmlNode by using XPath. Finally, we can call RemoveChild and pass in our instance of prideAndPrejudice. When that finishes, our books XmlNode will look like Figure 3-10.

33

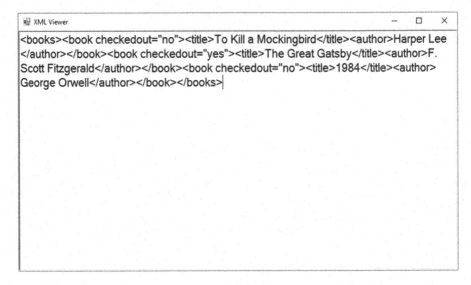

Figure 3-10. *Removing the book Pride and Prejudice*

Saving Our Changes

Once we have made our modifications, we need to ensure that these changes are written to disk. Using an instance of XmlDocument, we can just call the Save method and pass in the file name. Assuming we have made the changes to the library as well as having an instance of XmlDocument named doc, we just make the one call and we are done.

```
doc.Save("library-update.xml");
```

Our updated library looks as follows:

```
<?xml version="1.0"?>
<library xmlns:network="www.library.com">
  <books>
    <book checkedout="no">
      <title>To Kill a Mockingbird</title>
      <author>Harper Lee</author>
    </book>
    <book checkedout="no">
      <title>Price and Prejudice</title>
      <author>Jane Austen</author>
    </book>
    <book checkedout="yes">
      <title>The Great Gatsby</title>
      <author>F. Scott Fitzgerald</author>
    </book>
    <book checkedout="no">
```

```
    <title>1984</title>
    <author>George Orwell</author>
  </book>
  <book checkedout="no" damaged="no">
    <title>A Clockwork Orange</title>
    <year>1962</year>
  </book>
</books>
<movies>
  <movie checkedout="no">
    <title>King Kong</title>
    <year>1933</year>
  </movie>
  <movie checkedout="yes">
    <title>King Kong</title>
    <year>2005</year>
  </movie>
  <movie checkedout="yes">
    <title>To Kill A Mockingbird</title>
    <year>1962</year>
  </movie>
  <movie checkedout="no">
    <title>The Green Mile</title>
    <year>1999</year>
  </movie>
</movies>
</library>
```

LINQ to XML

Now let's try LINQ to XML.

Modifying Attributes

By using LINQ to XML, you are also able to modify attributes in a similar way to the XmlDocument. First, let's find all books that are currently checked out. (See Figure 3-11.)

```
XDocument library = XDocument.Load("library.xml");
IEnumerable<XElement> checkedOutBooks = library.Descendants()
    .Where(x => x.Name == "book"
    && x.Attribute("checkedout").Value == "yes");
```

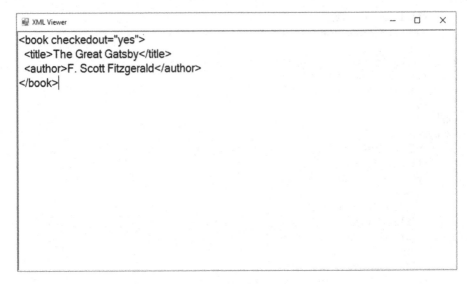

Figure 3-11. *The only book that has been checked out*

This will give us just one book, *The Great Gatsby*. Now let's say that for some reason all of the books have been returned to the library and there is not a single book out. By using LINQ to XML, we are able to not only get all of the books that are currently checked out but we can also modify the checkedout attribute so that it can show that we have no books checked out. (See Figure 3-12.)

```
XDocument library = XDocument.Load("library.xml");
IEnumerable<XElement> checkedOutBooks = library.Descendants()
    .Where(x => x.Name == "book" && x.Attribute("checkedout").Value == "yes");
foreach (XElement book in checkedOutBooks)
{
    book.Attribute("checkedout").Value = "no";
}
```

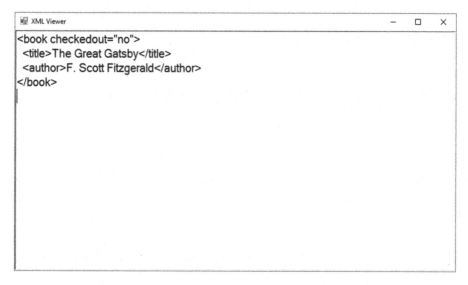

Figure 3-12. *Showing that the checkedout attribute has changed*

The above example only "checks in" one book since that is the only book that was checked out. This code allows us to check in as many books that are already checked out since it is pulling all books that are checked out and then iterating over them.

Modifying Elements

Just like modifying attributes in LINQ to XML, we are able to modify the elements. Modifying elements is similar to modifying the way we just modified the attributes. We just cut out the step to filter on the attribute. In this example, let's say that this library got rid of the original version of *The Green Mile* and then bought the "Director's Cut" version. We must update the catalog so that we have the latest version. We can use our trusty LINQ to XML to modify the title element:

```
XDocument library = XDocument.Load("library.xml");
XElement theGreenMile = library.Descendants()
    .Where(x => x.Name == "title" && x.Parent.Name == "movie" && x.Value ==
"The Green Mile").FirstOrDefault();
theGreenMile.Value = "The Green Mile (Director's Cut)";
```

Now we have a bit more magic going on in the code above. Notice that the Where method has three predicates instead of just two. We need to check three things in this example: the element name, the element parent name, and the element value. The reason we want to find the parent name is because we want to ensure that we are only modifying a movie. If we just used the prior criteria, we could modify a book as well. The code produces the output shown in Figure 3-13.

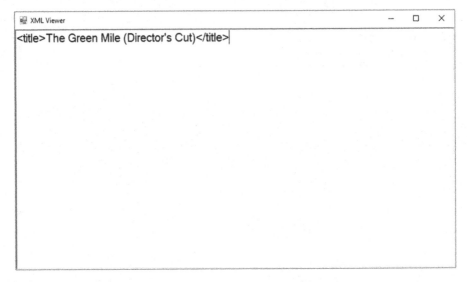

Figure 3-13. *The output from updating The Green Mile title*

Adding Attributes

Remember how we added a damaged attribute to the movies in the previous section? Well, let's add one to the books now using LINQ to XML:

```
XDocument library = XDocument.Load("library.xml");
IEnumerable<XElement> books = library.Descendants().Where(x => x.Name ==
"book");
foreach(XElement book in books)
{
    book.Add(new XAttribute("damaged", "no"));
}
```

Notice how easy it is to add an attribute using LINQ to XML. We add a new XAttribute instance and we can even instantiate it in the method since the constructor takes all the information needed for that attribute. You can see the output of this in Figure 3-14.

```
🖳 XML Viewer                                              —    □    ×

<book checkedout="no" damaged="no">
 <title>To Kill a Mockingbird</title>
 <author>Harper Lee</author>
</book><book checkedout="no" damaged="no">
 <title>Price and Prejudice</title>
 <author>Jane Austen</author>
</book><book checkedout="yes" damaged="no">
 <title>The Great Gatsby</title>
 <author>F. Scott Fitzgerald</author>
</book><book checkedout="no" damaged="no">
 <title>1984</title>
 <author>George Orwell</author>
</book>|
```

Figure 3-14. *Adding the damaged attribute*

Adding Elements

LINQ to XML keeps a very standard way of handling adding data to instances of XDocument by using the Add method. We are going to add another book to the library, but this time we will use LINQ to XML:

```
XDocument library = XDocument.Load("library.xml");
XElement books = library.Descendants().Where(x => x.Name == "books").
First();
XElement book = new XElement("book");
book.Add(new XElement("title", "The Cat in the Hat"));
book.Add(new XElement("author", "Dr. Seuss"));
books.Add(book);
```

We will first get the books element since we are adding a new book. Then we need to create an instance of XElement for our new book and we pass the element name in the constructor. One thing that is different from the XmlDocument is that in LINQ to XML you are able to instantiate XElements, as well as other classes, on their own without relying on the XmlDocument to create them. Once we have our book instantiated, we can go ahead and use the Add method to add our title and author. Because we only are going to have an element name and element value, we can just use the XElement constructor to instantiate an XElement class inside the Add method. It is possible to instantiate the XElement outside of the Add method, just as we did with the book variable. When all is said and done, we will end up with the output in Figure 3-15.

```
XML Viewer                                                        —   □   ×
<books>
 <book checkedout="no">
  <title>To Kill a Mockingbird</title>
  <author>Harper Lee</author>
 </book>
 <book checkedout="no">
  <title>Price and Prejudice</title>
  <author>Jane Austen</author>
 </book>
 <book checkedout="yes">
  <title>The Great Gatsby</title>
  <author>F. Scott Fitzgerald</author>
 </book>
 <book checkedout="no">
  <title>1984</title>
  <author>George Orwell</author>
 </book>
 <book>
  <title>The Cat in the Hat</title>
  <author>Dr. Seuss</author>
 </book>
</books>
```

Figure 3-15. *The books element after we added The Cat in the Hat book element*

Merging Documents

Microsoft not only made adding elements and attributes easy with LINQ to XML, it also made merging documents easy as well. We will revisit our example of two libraries and books moving between the two. We have our first library, which is what we have seen before and which we will call firstLibrary.

```xml
<?xml version="1.0"?>
<library xmlns:network="www.library.com">
        <books>
                <book checkedout="no">
                        <title>To Kill a Mockingbird</title>
                        <author>Harper Lee</author>
                </book>
                <book checkedout="no">
                        <title>Price and Prejudice</title>
                        <author>Jane Austen</author>
                </book>
                <book checkedout="yes">
                        <title>The Great Gatsby</title>
                        <author>F. Scott Fitzgerald</author>
                </book>
                <book checkedout="no">
                        <title>1984</title>
                        <author>George Orwell</author>
                </book>
```

```
        </books>
        <movies>
                <movie checkedout="no">
                        <title>King Kong</title>
                        <year>1933</year>
                </movie>
                <movie checkedout="yes">
                        <title>King Kong</title>
                        <year>2005</year>
                </movie>
                <movie checkedout="yes">
                        <title>To Kill A Mockingbird</title>
                        <year>1962</year>
                </movie>
                <movie checkedout="no">
                        <title>The Green Mile</title>
                        <year>1999</year>
                </movie>
        </movies>
</library>
```

But then we have the second library, which we will cleverly call secondLibrary.

```
<?xml version="1.0"?>
<library>
        <books>
                <book checkedout="no">
                        <title>To Kill a Mockingbird</title>
                        <author>Harper Lee</author>
                </book>
                <book checkedout="no">
                        <title>Price and Prejudice</title>
                        <author>Jane Austen</author>
                </book>
                <book checkedout="no">
                        <title>1984</title>
                        <author>George Orwell</author>
                </book>
        </books>
</library>
```

We want to move *The Great Gatsby* from firstLibrary to secondLibrary. We do this by first selecting the book element for *The Great Gatsby* from firstLibrary and then select the books element from secondLibrary. We can then use the Add method to add *The Great Gatsby* to the secondLibrary. When all is said and done, we will see the output in Figure 3-16.

```
XDocument firstLibrary = XDocument.Load("library.xml");
XElement gatsby = firstLibrary.Descendants()
    .Where(x => x.Name == "title" && x.Value == "The Great Gatsby")
    .Select(x => x.Parent).First();

XDocument secondLibrary = XDocument.Load("library2.xml");
XElement secondLibraryBooks = secondLibrary.Descendants()
    .Where(x => x.Name == "books").First();
secondLibraryBooks.Add(gatsby);
```

```
XML Viewer                                                    —    □    ×

<library>
 <books>
  <book checkedout="no">
   <title>To Kill a Mockingbird</title>
   <author>Harper Lee</author>
  </book>
  <book checkedout="no">
   <title>Price and Prejudice</title>
   <author>Jane Austen</author>
  </book>
  <book checkedout="no">
   <title>1984</title>
   <author>George Orwell</author>
  </book>
  <book checkedout="yes">
   <title>The Great Gatsby</title>
   <author>F. Scott Fitzgerald</author>
  </book>
 </books>
</library>
```

Figure 3-16. *The output from the second library after we add The Great Gatsby*

Removing Attributes

We have added attributes, but sometimes we want to remove them. For instance, if we are taking a book out of circulation in our library, we want to ensure that it isn't marked as checked out in our system. To do that, we can remove the attribute. The way to remove an attribute is not as straightforward as when we add one. We need to use the Remove method, but it isn't on the XElement instance. Instead, it is on the XAttribute instance.

```
XDocument library = XDocument.Load("library.xml");
XElement theGreatGatsby = library.Descendants()
    .Where(x => x.Name == "title" && x.Value == "The Great Gatsby")
    .Select(x => x.Parent).First();
XAttribute checkedout = theGreatGatsby.Attributes("checkedout").First();
checkedout.Remove();
```

As always, in order to get the attributes, we need to get the book element so we search for *The Great Gatsby*. When we find it, we use the Attributes method on the XElement instance. If we pass in a name, then it will get a IEnumerable of all the XAttributes with that name. If we don't pass in a name, it will give us an IEnumerable of all the attributes. Since we only want one attribute, we will search for checkedout and then get the first instance. That will return an instance of XAttribute that represents the checkedout attribute. It is on this instance that we must call Remove. Once we do that, we get the output in Figure 3-17.

Figure 3-17. *The Great Gatsby after we remove the checkedout attribute*

Removing Elements

To continue our example of pulling *The Great Gatsby* out of circulation in our library, we need to remove the book element that represents *The Great Gatsby* from the library.

```
XDocument library = XDocument.Load("library.xml");
XElement theGreatGatsby = library.Descendants()
    .Where(x => x.Name == "title" && x.Value == "The Great Gatsby")
    .Select(x => x.Parent).First();
theGreatGatsby.Remove();
```

The way we remove the instance of the XElement that represents *The Great Gatsby* is the same method we used to remove an attribute: Remove. Just like the attribute example, we get an instance of the object we want to remove (in this case, the XElement instance that represents *The Great Gatsby*) and then just call the Remove method. While it isn't as intuitive as adding attributes or elements, being able to remove attributes and elements is consistent across all LINQ to XML types.

Saving Our Changes

Once we have made all of our changes, we need to save the XDocument instance back to an XML file. In order to do that with LINQ to XML, just like with the XmlDocument, all we need to do to save is call the Save method. After we save the changes we made by removing *The Great Gatsby*, our XML looks like the following.

```
<?xml version="1.0" encoding="utf-8"?>
<library xmlns:network="www.library.com">
  <books>
    <book checkedout="no">
      <title>To Kill a Mockingbird</title>
      <author>Harper Lee</author>
    </book>
    <book checkedout="no">
      <title>Price and Prejudice</title>
      <author>Jane Austen</author>
    </book>
    <book checkedout="no">
      <title>1984</title>
      <author>George Orwell</author>
    </book>
  </books>
  <movies>
    <movie checkedout="no">
      <title>King Kong</title>
      <year>1933</year>
    </movie>
    <movie checkedout="yes">
      <title>King Kong</title>
      <year>2005</year>
    </movie>
    <movie checkedout="yes">
      <title>To Kill A Mockingbird</title>
      <year>1962</year>
    </movie>
    <movie checkedout="no">
      <title>The Green Mile</title>
      <year>1999</year>
    </movie>
  </movies>
</library>
```

CHAPTER 4

Serialization

There are times when your program is the only program handling the XML, such as a configuration file or some sort of XML datastore. In times like those, it can be tedious to use LINQ to XML or the XmlDocument to load, manipulate, and save your XML, especially since you know exactly what there is. If this is the case, then you can use serialization to save and read your XML. As I indicated earlier, this technique is only proper if you are the only one using this XML document.

Creating a Model

Before you are able to serialize your XML, there has to be a model first. Serialization is completely attribute based, so you do not need to do anything but add the attributes to your class and what you wish to serialize. We will continue the library theme that was presented in the previous chapters by creating a book model to serialize.

```
[Serializable]
public class Book
{
    public string Title { get; set; }
    public string Author { get; set; }
    public DateTime Year { get; set; }
}
```

Because there is the Serializable attribute on this book class that notifies the serializer that this class will be serialized when passed in to the XML serializer, you will need to include the System.Xml.Serialization namespace to use the XmlSerializer.

Writing to File

Setting the serializer to write to file can seem daunting at first. After all, you will have to use multiple streams. Once you pass that learning bump, it isn't bad at all. It still requires less code than the methods we have previously gone over. Following is an example of writing our book class to file:

© Jonathan Hartwell 2017
J. Hartwell, *C# and XML Primer*, DOI 10.1007/978-1-4842-2595-0_4

```
Book book = new Book()
{
    Title = "Gone With the Wind",
    Year = 1937,
    Author = "Margaret Mitchell"
};
XmlSerializer serializer = new XmlSerializer(typeof(Book), "");
using (MemoryStream stream = new MemoryStream())
{
    serializer.Serialize(stream, book);

    using (FileStream fs = new FileStream("book.xml", FileMode.Create))
    {
        stream.WriteTo(fs);
        fs.Flush();
    }
}
```

We first create a new instance of our book model and populate the fields. Once we do that, we need to instantiate our XmlSerializer class. The constructor I chose to use takes a type and a default namespace. Because a type is required as the first argument, we must use the typeof construct in C# with the class name of the model we are serializing. We then pass in a default namespace that we want to be used. In this example, I pass in an empty string as we don't need a namespace. Once we have our serializer, we get to the fun part—dealing with streams. In this example, we are writing to file, but since this uses streams, you could write to any stream that performs any sort of peristance or reading. In order to load our MemoryStream, however, we need to populate a byte array. We can use the length property in order to instantiate our byte array with the exact size of the stream. Since we want to write to file, we have to instantiate our FileStream. We want to create the file and write to "book.xml". Once we have our instance of FileStream, we are able to write our instance of MemoryStream directly into the file stream. After the FileStream instance has the contents of the MemoryStream instance, we need to call the Flush method on our FileStream instance so we can persist the data to a file. After the data is flushed, we get a book.xml file that looks like the following XML:

```
<?xml version="1.0"?>
<Book xmlns:xsi="http://www.w3.org/2001/XMLSchema-instance"
xmlns:xsd="http://www.w3.org/2001/XMLSchema">
  <Title>Gone With the Wind</Title>
  432799_1_EnMargaret Mitchell</Author>
  <Year>1937</Year>
</Book>
```

The XML looks no different than what we would have created using XmlDocument or LINQ to XML, yet it took only a few lines of code to do so. You may have noticed the namespaces on the Book element. Since those are typically the default namespaces, the XmlSerializer will add those to the root element. Another thing to note is that the root element is the name of our model type.

So how does this work under the hood? The XmlSerializer uses reflection to get the properties of a given serializable class and then creates elements based on those properties. Since this is all handled by reflection, there are several attributes that can be used to iterate on that will perform various actions. For instance, there is the XmlAttribute class, which is used on a property that should have some sort of attributes. There is also an XmlIgnore attribute, which can be used to indicate that a specific property should not be serialized. In Chapter 5, we will create our own XmlSerializer so that we can get a better understanding of exactly how it works.

I just gave examples of other attributes that can be used in a given model. Let's use both of them and see what the output is. We will revisit our book model again. This time, let's not serialize the year that the book was written and let's also add a propety to the name to indicate that a movie has been made based on this book. Our Book class now changes to the following model:

```
[Serializable]
public class Book
{
    [XmlAttribute(AttributeName = "Movie")]
    public bool IsMovie { get; set; }
    public string Title { get; set; }

    public string Author { get; set; }

    [XmlIgnore]
    public int Year;
}
```

We added a new property, IsMovie, which will indicate whether the movie has been made. We also used the XmlAttribute attribute to indicate that the IsMovie property will be an attribute on the Book element. We use the AttributeName property on the XmlAttribute constructor to pass in our attribute name. Take note that we named our property IsMovie, but we are calling it something different in our attribute. It may not make sense to call the attribute the same name as our property. Variable names in C# can be quite long as they describe what they are for and make it easier for the programmer to understand what is happening. However, when it comes to XML, being clear but terse is much preferred as it keeps the document smaller but still conveys the point. You may have noticed that there is a change in the Year member of the Book class. When we run the serializer on the above code, we end up with the following output:

```
<?xml version="1.0"?>
<Book xmlns:xsi="http://www.w3.org/2001/XMLSchema-instance"
xmlns:xsd="http://www.w3.org/2001/XMLSchema" Movie="true">
  <Title>Gone With the Wind</Title>
  432799_1_EnMargaret Mitchell</Author>
</Book>
```

Everything looks pretty much the same with the exception of the Movie attribute on the Book element as well as the Year element is missing. XML does not have a concept of boolean so when we use a boolean as a propety, the output will be either "true" or "false," both as strings. The serialization process looks exactly the same, too.

```
Book book = new Book()
{
    Title = "Gone With the Wind",
    Year = 1937,
    Author = "Margaret Mitchell",
    IsMovie = true
};
XmlSerializer serializer = new XmlSerializer(typeof(Book), "");
using (MemoryStream stream = new MemoryStream())
{
    serializer.Serialize(stream, book);
    byte[] buffer = new byte[stream.Length];

    using (FileStream fs = new FileStream("book.xml", FileMode.Create))
    {
        stream.WriteTo(fs);
        fs.Flush();
    }
}
```

There are many more attributes that we can use to modify the output of our XML. We have already seen Ignore and XmlAttribute, but what if we want our class to have text instead of nested elements? We could change our model to include the XmlText attribute, which will make the value of a property the text of the given class instead of its own element.

```
[Serializable]
public class Book
{
    [XmlAttribute(AttributeName = "Movie")]
    public bool IsMovie { get; set; }
    public string Title { get; set; }
    [XmlText]
    public string Author { get; set; }

    [XmlIgnore]
    public int Year { get; set; }

}
```

We have put the XML text attribute on our Author property. Instead of creating an author element, we will get text that we can see in the following output:

```xml
<?xml version="1.0"?>
<Book xmlns:xsi="http://www.w3.org/2001/XMLSchema-instance"
xmlns:xsd="http://www.w3.org/2001/XMLSchema" Movie="false">
        <Title>Gone With the Wind</Title>Margaret Mitchell</Book>
```

We have now see the typical properties such as string and int, but there can be other types that we would want to serialize, such as an enumeration.

If we add an enum to our project as well as add the enum as a property on our Book class, we serialize that class again and we get pretty much what would be expected.

```csharp
[Serializable]
public class Book
{
    [XmlAttribute(AttributeName = "Movie")]
    public bool IsMovie { get; set; }
    public string Title { get; set; }
    [XmlText]
    public string Author { get; set; }

    [XmlIgnore]
    public int Year { get; set; }

    public Color Color { get; set; }

}

public enum Color
{
    Black,
    Red
}
```

```xml
<?xml version="1.0"?>
<Book xmlns:xsi="http://www.w3.org/2001/XMLSchema-instance"
xmlns:xsd="http://www.w3.org/2001/XMLSchema" Movie="false">
   <Title>Gone With the Wind</Title>Margaret Mitchell<Color>Black</Color></
Book>
```

So you may be asking yourself why we would need attributes for enumerations if we are already getting exactly what would be expected. But what if we change the enumeration to a number instead of the text of the color?

```csharp
public enum Color
{
    One,
    Two
}
```

Now, this is not a great design as it makes it confusing, but we can pretend that this is legacy code that we have to take over. We can take a look at the output that this will now produce:

```
<?xml version="1.0"?>
<Book xmlns:xsi="http://www.w3.org/2001/XMLSchema-instance"
xmlns:xsd="http://www.w3.org/2001/XMLSchema" Movie="false">
  <Title>Gone With the Wind</Title>Margaret Mitchell<Color>One</Color></
Book>
```

We see the value of the Color element is now One. But what does that mean? If we were to change all of the enumeration values that could break a lot of code, how do we get a readable XML output without causing possible issues? Simple. We use the XmlEnum attribute.

```
public enum Color
{
    [XmlEnum(Name ="Black")]
    One,
    [XmlEnum(Name ="Red")]
    Two
}
```

We have used the XmlEnum attribute and given the Name property our color value. This will now give us the proper output that we were originally expecting:

```
<?xml version="1.0"?>
<Book xmlns:xsi="http://www.w3.org/2001/XMLSchema-instance"
xmlns:xsd="http://www.w3.org/2001/XMLSchema" Movie="false">
  <Title>Gone With the Wind</Title>Margaret Mitchell<Color>Black</Color></
Book>
```

For our Color enum, we gave both values an XmlEnum attribute, but there is no rule saying that both of our values must have an attribute. We could also do something like the following:

```
public enum Color
{
    [XmlEnum(Name ="Black")]
    One,
    Two
}
```

We now have our Color values of One and Two but only have an attribute on our One value. It should not be a surprise on what our output is, but our Color element is now Two when we set the Color attribute to two:

```xml
<?xml version="1.0"?>
<Book xmlns:xsi="http://www.w3.org/2001/XMLSchema-instance"
xmlns:xsd="http://www.w3.org/2001/XMLSchema" Movie="false">
  <Title>Gone With the Wind</Title>Margaret Mitchell<Color>Two</Color></
Book>
```

Composition

Up until now, we have only dealt with one class, Book. In the real world, you will have to serialize more than just one class, and some classes will have other classes as members and may even have collections of types as a member. Remember the previous chapters where we had a library? Well, let's revisit this example with serialization.

First, let's do a simple example of a library that has only one book:

```
[Serializable]
public class Library
{
    public Book Classic;
}
```

We have our library class that will also need to have the serializable attribute. We then add our Book class as a member. We do need to tweak our code to serialize in order to compensate for the change to our model structure.

```
Book book = new Book()
{
    Title = "Gone With the Wind",
    Year = 1937,
    Author = "Margaret Mitchell",
    Color = Color.Two
};
Library library = new Library() { Classic = book };
XmlSerializer serializer = new XmlSerializer(typeof(Library), "");
using (MemoryStream stream = new MemoryStream())
{
    serializer.Serialize(stream, library);
    byte[] buffer = new byte[stream.Length];

    using (FileStream fs = new FileStream("library.xml", FileMode.Create))
    {
        stream.WriteTo(fs);
        fs.Flush();
    }
}
```

Our change in this case was to just create an instance of Library and then change all of the serialize code that references the Book class as well as instance of our Book class to the Library class.

Now that we have created an instance of our Library class and added a book to it, we can use the code above to serialize our library.

```
<?xml version="1.0"?>
<Library xmlns:xsi="http://www.w3.org/2001/XMLSchema-instance"
xmlns:xsd="http://www.w3.org/2001/XMLSchema">
  <Classic Movie="false">
    <Title>Gone With the Wind</Title>
    432799_1_EnMargaret Mitchell</Author>
    <Color>Two</Color>
  </Classic>
</Library>
```

If you take a look at the XML that was outputted by our new code, you may notice something is a bit off. Instead of the library having a Book element, it has a Classic element. Remember our output of our Book class serialization? All the elements were the name of the property name and not the type of the property. This is no different as it will output the property name. Have no fear. We can change that. After all, it doesn't make much sense to have an element named Classic in our library since not all books are classics. We are able to use another attribute, XmlElement.

XmlElement is an attribute that allows you to change the name of a property that is a member of a given class that has the Serializable attribute. Our library model now has an extra attribute.

```
[Serializable]
public class Library
{
    [XmlElement(ElementName ="Book")]
    public Book Classic;
}
```

When we serialize this new version of the Library class, we can get XML output that is what we expect.

```
<?xml version="1.0"?>
<Library xmlns:xsi="http://www.w3.org/2001/XMLSchema-instance"
xmlns:xsd="http://www.w3.org/2001/XMLSchema">
  <Book Movie="false">
    <Title>Gone With the Wind</Title>
    432799_1_EnMargaret Mitchell</Author>
    <Color>Two</Color>
  </Book>
</Library>
```

We are also able to make element name modifications to the Library class. Since we are declaring Library as a class and not a property, we are not able to use the XmlElement attribute. However, we are provided with another attribute that allows us to modify our Library element name: XmlRoot. Since the Library class is the root of our XML document, using the XmlRoot attribute makes sense. It is used similarly to the XmlElement attribute where we can pass the ElementName property through the constructor. Let's say that we want our Library XML to describe a university library. Our model and output will now look like the following:

```
[Serializable]
[XmlRoot(ElementName ="UniversityLibrary")]
public class Library
{
    [XmlElement(ElementName ="Book")]
    public Book Classic;
}
<?xml version="1.0"?>
<UniversityLibrary xmlns:xsi="http://www.w3.org/2001/XMLSchema-instance"
xmlns:xsd="http://www.w3.org/2001/XMLSchema">
  <Book Movie="false">
    <Title>Gone With the Wind</Title>
    432799_1_EnMargaret Mitchell</Author>
    <Color>Two</Color>
  </Book>
</UniversityLibrary>
```

While some classes have a single property that may need to be serialized, it doesn't make sense for a library to have just one book. To fix that, we can make a list of books. Our library model now looks like the following:

```
[Serializable]
[XmlRoot(ElementName ="UniversityLibrary")]
public class Library
{
    public List<Book> Books { get; set; }

    public Library()
    {
        Books = new List<Book>();
    }
}
```

Now that we have the list, we are ready to serialize the entire library. We don't need to make a single change to how we serialize. We can use the code that we originally used to serialize our library. The output XML ends up being similar to what we had seen when we were writing our XML in the previous chapter.

```
<?xml version="1.0"?>
<UniversityLibrary xmlns:xsi="http://www.w3.org/2001/XMLSchema-instance"
xmlns:xsd="http://www.w3.org/2001/XMLSchema">
  <Books>
    <Book Movie="false">
      <Title>Gone With the Wind</Title>
      432799_1_EnMargaret Mitchell</Author>
      <Color>Two</Color>
    </Book>
    <Book Movie="false">
      <Title>Pride and Prejudice</Title>
      432799_1_EnJane Austen</Author>
      <Color>Black</Color>
    </Book>
  </Books>
</UniversityLibrary>
```

Let's say that we don't want to use the name books. If we had a model class that had a list that was named BookList, we wouldn't want the top level element named BookList. We also cannot use the XmlElement attribute on a list because that will apply the XmlElement attribute to all items in the list. We would still have "BookList" as the top level element, but all of the children would have the name given in the XmlElement attribute. In order to change the container element name, we have to use the XmlArray attribute. We can change the Library class so that it takes advantage of the XmlArray attribute, which would give us the following XML output:

```
[Serializable]
[XmlRoot(ElementName ="UniversityLibrary")]
public class Library
{

    [XmlArray(ElementName = "Classics")]
    public List<Book> Books { get; set; }

    public Library()
    {
        Books = new List<Book>();
    }
}
```

```
<?xml version="1.0"?>
<UniversityLibrary xmlns:xsi="http://www.w3.org/2001/XMLSchema-instance"
xmlns:xsd="http://www.w3.org/2001/XMLSchema">
  <Classics>
    <Book Movie="false">
      <Title>Gone With the Wind</Title>
      432799_1_EnMargaret Mitchell</Author>
      <Color>Two</Color>
    </Book>
```

```
    <Book Movie="false">
      <Title>Pride and Prejudice</Title>
      432799_1_EnJane Austen</Author>
      <Color>Black</Color>
    </Book>
  </Classics>
</UniversityLibrary>
```

Inheritance

Sometimes there are instances where it is appropriate to create a class that inherits from another class. That is no problem normally, but it can cause issues when trying to serialize XML. We can add a class named Classic that will inherit from the Book class. Our model classes will now look as follows:

```
[Serializable]
public class Book
{
    [XmlAttribute(AttributeName = "Movie")]
    public bool IsMovie { get; set; }
    public string Title { get; set; }
    public string Author { get; set; }

    [XmlIgnore]
    public int Year { get; set; }

    public Color Color { get; set; }

}

[Serializable]
[XmlRoot(ElementName = "UniversityLibrary")]
public class Library
{

    [XmlArray(ElementName = "Classics")]
    public List<Book> Books { get; set; }

    public Library()
    {
        Books = new List<Book>();
    }
}

public class Classic : Book
{

}
```

55

If we do a straight replace with changing one of the Book classes that are added the Library instance of the List<Book>, we will get an error, System. InvalidOperationException, as shown in Figure 4-1.

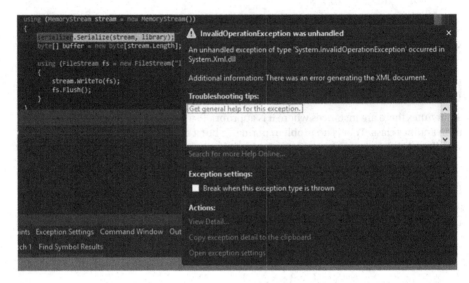

Figure 4-1. *The error ouput of when initially using the Classic class and serializing*

The reason that we get this error is because our Library class does not know anything about the Classic class. After all, we are only declaring a List of Book type and while Classic inherits from Book, it isn't a Book. In order for this to work, we need to go ahead and add the XmlInclude attribute on the Library class. That attribute requires a type to be passed into the constructor, so we will pass in the type of Classic.

```
[Serializable]
[XmlRoot(ElementName = "UniversityLibrary")]
[XmlInclude(typeof(Classic))]
public class Library
{

    [XmlArray(ElementName = "Classics")]

    public List<Book> Books { get; set; }

    public Library()
    {
        Books = new List<Book>();
    }
}
```

Once we add the XmlInclude attribute, the program can run and correctly serialize the instance of Library to XML. The output is a bit different from what we have seen before.

```
<?xml version="1.0"?>
<UniversityLibrary xmlns:xsi="http://www.w3.org/2001/XMLSchema-instance"
xmlns:xsd="http://www.w3.org/2001/XMLSchema">
  <Classics>
    <Book Movie="false">
      <Title>Gone With the Wind</Title>
      432799_1_EnMargaret Mitchell</Author>
      <Color>Two</Color>
    </Book>
    <Book xsi:type="Classic" Movie="false">
      <Title>Pride and Prejudice</Title>
      432799_1_EnJane Austen</Author>
      <Color>Black</Color>
    </Book>
  </Classics>
</UniversityLibrary>
```

All the content looks the same, but there is an attribute on the Book that has the title *Pride and Prejudice*. There is the xsi:type attribute that contains the value Classic. This lets the serializer know that this type is not just a Book class but actually a Classic class. Notice that the Year property is missing from the Book and the Classic elements. We put the XmlIgnore attribute on the Year property in the Book class and, since we inherited the Classic class from Book, all of the attributes are kept intact for the instances of Classic.

Let's say that we now want to track if a Classic book is paperback or not. After all, this could potentially affect the cost of that book. We will add a Paperback property of type bool on the Classic class.

```
public class Classic : Book
{
    public bool Paperback { get; set; }
}
```

We can then run the program to generate the XML and we can see that there is an added element to the Book with Classic attribute that is not on the regular Book element.

```
<?xml version="1.0"?>
<UniversityLibrary xmlns:xsi="http://www.w3.org/2001/XMLSchema-instance"
xmlns:xsd="http://www.w3.org/2001/XMLSchema">
  <Classics>
    <Book Movie="false">
      <Title>Gone With the Wind</Title>
      432799_1_EnMargaret Mitchell</Author>
      <Color>Two</Color>
    </Book>
```

```
    <Book xsi:type="Classic" Movie="false">
      <Title>Pride and Prejudice</Title>
      432799_1_EnJane Austen</Author>
      <Color>Black</Color>
      <Paperback>false</Paperback>
    </Book>
  </Classics>
</UniversityLibrary>
```

SOAP

Once you have the hang of serializing XML with XmlSerializer and XmlDeserializer, you can use them to handle SOAP. *SOAP* stands for *Simple Object Access Protocol* and is used in Web services that use XML as a stream. In order to be able to serialize a class in the SOAP format, we have to use a few specialized attributes. Let's first look at the new class we are going to use for our SOAP serialization:

```
[SoapType("SoapBook", "http://www.apress.com")]
public class SoapBook
{
    public string Title { get; set; }
}
```

This is a simple class that contains just one property, Title, but we have a new attribute on the class. The SoapType attribute takes a name and namespace. The name parameter is what the root element on the XML document will be called. Using this new class, we can generate the SOAP XML using a modified version of the code we have used.

```
SoapBook book = new SoapBook()
{
    Title = "Test"
};
XmlTypeMapping mapping = (new SoapReflectionImporter().ImportTypeMapping(ty
peof(SoapBook)));
XmlSerializer serializer = new XmlSerializer(mapping);
using (MemoryStream stream = new MemoryStream())
{
    serializer.Serialize(stream, book);
    byte[] buffer = new byte[stream.Length];

    using (FileStream fs = new FileStream("soap.xml", FileMode.Create))
    {
        stream.WriteTo(fs);
        fs.Flush();
    }
}
```

There are two things that we need to change in order for us to be able to serialize this class in a SOAP format. First, we need to create an instance of XmlTypeMapping class. To instantiate this class, there is a complex-looking constructor. We need to declare a new SoapReflectionImporter class and then call the ImportTypeMapping method. That method takes a type as a parameter so we need to give the method of our new class. We then pass that XmlTypeMapping instance, mapping, into the XmlSerializer constructor. From then on, we do everything the exact same way. This will provide the following XML:

```
<?xml version="1.0"?>
<q1:SoapBook xmlns:xsi="http://www.w3.org/2001/XMLSchema-instance"
xmlns:xsd="http://www.w3.org/2001/XMLSchema" id="id1" xmlns:q1="http://www.
apress.com">
  <Title xsi:type="xsd:string">Test</Title>
</q1:SoapBook>
```

This is what a typical SOAP request will look like. There are the default namespaces xsi and xsd, but then there is our namespace, q1, which is what we passed into the SoapType attribute constructor. Our classes will have the namespace prefix q1 while the xsi prefix will be used for the type attribute and the xsd namespace will be used to declare types. Our Title element has a type of string according to this XML, which is exactly what we passed in.

There are attributes that are used in the typical XML serialization that has a specialized version for SOAP. If we wanted to ignore a property for serialization, we would use XmlIgnore, but if we use it with SOAP, then it wouldn't have any effect, as demonstrated below. We will add a new property to our SoapBook class and then put an XmlIgnore on that property.

```
[SoapType("SoapBook", "http://www.apress.com")]
public class SoapBook
{

    public string Title { get; set; }
    [XmlIgnore]
    public int Year { get; set; }
}
```

When we run that through the modified code to handle the SOAP serialization, we have the following output:

```
<?xml version="1.0"?>
<q1:SoapBook xmlns:xsi="http://www.w3.org/2001/XMLSchema-instance"
xmlns:xsd="http://www.w3.org/2001/XMLSchema" id="id1" xmlns:q1="http://www.
apress.com">
  <Title xsi:type="xsd:string">Test</Title>
  <Year xsi:type="xsd:int">2016</Year>
</q1:SoapBook>
```

Notice that the Year property is still in the output despite having the XmlIgnore attribute. That is because we must use the SOAP version of the ignore, SoapIgnore. Once we use that attribute, the Year element will drop off the XML output.

We are able to make complex SOAP objects, meaning classes that have other classes that we created as members, but it completely changes the way that we have to write the code to serialize. There are many gotchas when trying to use the code we have already written and just adding the complex classes we are serializing into the mix. But first, let's take a look at the changes we made to our SoapBook class and what we have added to the new SoapLibrary class.

```
[SoapType("Book", "http://www.apress.com/Book")]
public class SoapBook
{
    [SoapElement("Title")]
    public string Title { get; set; }
    [SoapIgnore]
    public int Year { get; set; }
}

[SoapType("Library","http://www.apress.com/Library")]
public class SoapLibrary
{
    public List<SoapBook> Books { get; set; }
}
```

There are a few changes that we made. First, we added the SoapLibrary class that has a List of SoapBook as a member. But we also changed the namespace for the SoapBook class as well to the SoapLibrary class. For each class that we create, we must create a new namespace for that class. No two classe are able to have the same namespace. Before we get to the code, let's take a look at the output, which is not valid XML but contains all of the information that will be outputted by the XML serializer in our new version of code.

```
<q1:Library xmlns:xsi="http://www.w3.org/2001/XMLSchema-instance"
xmlns:xsd="http://www.w3.org/2001/XMLSchema" id="id1" xmlns:q1="http://www.
apress.com/Library">
                <Books href="#id2" />
        </q1:Library>
        <q2:Array id="id2" xmlns:q3="http://www.apress.com/Book"
q2:arrayType="q3:Book[1]" xmlns:q2="http://schemas.xmlsoap.org/soap/
encoding/">
                <Item href="#id3" />
        </q2:Array>
        <q4:Book id="id3" p2:type="q4:Book" xmlns:p2="http://www.
w3.org/2001/XMLSchema-instance" xmlns:q4="http://www.apress.com/Book">
                <Title xmlns:q5="http://www.w3.org/2001/XMLSchema"
p2:type="q5:string">Pride and Prejudice</Title>
        </q4:Book>
```

You can see why this is not valid XML as there is no root element; all of the classes are in their own element that sits at the same level as each of the other classes. If you look at the id attribute and the href attributes, you can see how these items fit together. The first element that we see is the Library element, which represents the SoapLibrary class. The SoapLibrary class has a member property that is a List of SoapBooks that is represented by the property Books. We can see that the child of the Library element is the Books element. It has an href attribute attached to it that is #id2. That href refers to an element that has the id attribute id2. In this case, that happens to be the Array element that is below the Library element. This Array element has information regarding the Books list. First, it has the arrayType attribute, which shows the namespace of the Book element as well as the number of Book elements that appear in this array. There is also the id attribute of id2. We now know that the Book element that is a child of Library is referenced by this specific Array element.

If you take a look at the child of the Array element, you will see that there is an Item element. This element has an href attribute of #id3, which means it is referencing the element with the id attribute that is equal to id3. Taking a look at the rest of the XML document, we find that the Book element has the id of id3. That means that the Item element is referring to that book. That book also has a child Title element, which contains the actual title of this book. There is a lot of work when we try to work our way through this XML document. But that isn't the only work that needs to be done.

As I mentioned before, there needs to be a different approach in order to generate this XML.

```
SoapBook book = new SoapBook()
{
    Title = "Pride and Prejudice",
    Year = 1813
};

SoapLibrary lib = new SoapLibrary()
{
    Books = new List<SoapBook>() { book }
};
XmlTypeMapping mapping = (new SoapReflectionImporter().ImportTypeMapping(typ
eof(SoapLibrary)));

XmlSerializer serializer = new XmlSerializer(mapping);

using (FileStream fs = new FileStream("soap.xml", FileMode.Create))
{
    using (XmlWriter writer = XmlWriter.Create(fs))
    {
        writer.WriteStartElement("Root");
        serializer.Serialize(writer, lib);
        writer.WriteEndElement();
    }
}
```

We start by declaring our SoapBook instance like we have done in the past. After that, we instantiate our SoapLibrary class and add the SoapBook instance to the List of SoapBooks. We then create the XmlTypeMapping using the type of SoapLibrary and from there create our instance of the XmlSerializer class. So far, this has been the exact same way that we have handled XmlSerialization in the past, but now we get to the part of the code that is different.

Instead of using an instance of MemoryStream, we are going to create an instance of FileStream where we pass in the name of our XML document that will be saved to file. We then instantiate an XmlWriter class and pass in the FileStream instance that we have already created. We are going to write all of the information to the FileStream via the XmlWriter. Remember how I mentioned that the output from before was not proper XML and that is because it lacked a root? Well, we need to use the XmlWriter method WriteStartElement() to create an element that we will call Root. Once the element is created, we can finally serialize our SOAP objects by calling the Serialize method on the XmlSerializer. After we are done serializing, we need to close our Root element by calling WriteEndElement and we are done serializing. Because we are handling the streams by using statements, we do not need to call save or flush on the FileStream instance as that is handled for us. Our XML output is as follows:

```
<?xml version="1.0" encoding="utf-8"?>
<Root>
        <q1:Library xmlns:xsi="http://www.w3.org/2001/XMLSchema-instance"
xmlns:xsd="http://www.w3.org/2001/XMLSchema" id="id1" xmlns:q1="http://www.
apress.com/Library">
                <Books href="#id2" />
        </q1:Library>
        <q2:Array id="id2" xmlns:q3="http://www.apress.com/Book"
q2:arrayType="q3:Book[1]" xmlns:q2="http://schemas.xmlsoap.org/soap/
encoding/">
                <Item href="#id3" />
        </q2:Array>
        <q4:Book id="id3" p2:type="q4:Book" xmlns:p2="http://www.
w3.org/2001/XMLSchema-instance" xmlns:q4="http://www.apress.com/Book">
                <Title xmlns:q5="http://www.w3.org/2001/XMLSchema"
p2:type="q5:string">Pride and Prejudice</Title>
        </q4:Book>
</Root>
```

We have the same XML that was shown before, but now there is a root element that allows us to have proper formatted XML. A few paragraphs ago, I said that we had to change the way we handled the XML. Well, there is a good reason why. We can get 99% of the way to the proper results by using our old method, but we just can't get that 1% to finish.

```
SoapBook book = new SoapBook()
{
    Title = "Pride and Prejudice",
    Year = 1813
};
```

```
SoapLibrary lib = new SoapLibrary()
{
    Books = new List<SoapBook>() { book }
};
XmlTypeMapping mapping = (new SoapReflectionImporter().ImportTypeMapping(typ
eof(SoapLibrary)));

XmlSerializer serializer = new XmlSerializer(mapping);

using (MemoryStream stream = new MemoryStream())
{
    using (XmlWriter writer = XmlWriter.Create(stream))
    {
        writer.WriteStartElement("Root");
        serializer.Serialize(writer, lib);
        writer.WriteEndElement();
        using (FileStream fs = new FileStream("soap.xml", FileMode.Create))
        {
            stream.WriteTo(fs);
            fs.Flush();
        }

    }
}
```

We need a root element, so I just included the XmlWriter instance in order to create that element. If we do not do that, then we won't even be able to serialize to file as the Serialize method will throw an exception. When we run this code, we do get an XML document, but it is not valid.

```
<?xml version="1.0" encoding="utf-8"?>
<Root>
        <q1:Library xmlns:xsi="http://www.w3.org/2001/XMLSchema-instance"
xmlns:xsd="http://www.w3.org/2001/XMLSchema" id="id1" xmlns:q1="http://www.
apress.com/Library">
                <Books href="#id2" />
        </q1:Library>
        <q2:Array id="id2" xmlns:q3="http://www.apress.com/Book"
q2:arrayType="q3:Book[1]" xmlns:q2="http://schemas.xmlsoap.org/soap/
encoding/">
                <Item href="#id3" />
        </q2:Array>
        <q4:Book id="id3" p2:type="q4:Book" xmlns:p2="http://www.
w3.org/2001/XMLSchema-instance" xmlns:q4="http://www.apress.com/Book">
                <Title xmlns:q5="http://www.w3.org/2001/XMLSchema"
p2:type="q5:string">Pride and Prejudice</Title>
        </q4:Book>
```

Can you tell what is missing? I'll give you a hint—check for closing tags. That's right. There is an open tag for Root, but it never closes. Once we serialize to the instance of XmlWriter, we are unable to make any changes to that stream, meaning that we are unable to add a closing tag for our Root element.

We have only given a relatively simple example of outputing SOAP up until now. We have a List of SoapBook types, but we only put one instance in that list. Typically, when we have an instance of a list, we have more than one item in that list. So let's go over the code again, but this time we will put multiple instances of SoapBook in our list.

```
SoapBook book = new SoapBook()
{
    Title = "Pride and Prejudice",
    Year = 1813
};

SoapBook book2 = new SoapBook()
{
    Title = "To Kill a Mockingbird",
    Year = 1960
};

SoapLibrary lib = new SoapLibrary()
{
    Books = new List<SoapBook>() { book,book2 }
};
XmlTypeMapping mapping = (new SoapReflectionImporter().ImportTypeMapping
(typeof(SoapLibrary))

XmlSerializer serializer = new XmlSerializer(mapping);

using (FileStream fs = new FileStream("soap.xml", FileMode.Create))
{
    using (XmlWriter writer = XmlWriter.Create(fs))
    {
        writer.WriteStartElement("Root");
        serializer.Serialize(writer, lib);
        writer.WriteEndElement();
    }
}
```

Now, when we run this program, we will get a more complex XML document.

```
<?xml version="1.0" encoding="utf-8"?>
<Root>
        <q1:Library xmlns:xsi="http://www.w3.org/2001/XMLSchema-instance"
xmlns:xsd="http://www.w3.org/2001/XMLSchema" id="id1" xmlns:q1="http://www.
apress.com/Library">
                <Books href="#id2" />
```

```
        </q1:Library>
        <q2:Array id="id2" xmlns:q3="http://www.apress.com/Book"
q2:arrayType="q3:Book[2]" xmlns:q2="http://schemas.xmlsoap.org/soap/
encoding/">
                <Item href="#id3" />
                <Item href="#id4" />
        </q2:Array>
        <q4:Book id="id3" p2:type="q4:Book" xmlns:p2="http://www.
w3.org/2001/XMLSchema-instance" xmlns:q4="http://www.apress.com/Book">
                <Title xmlns:q5="http://www.w3.org/2001/XMLSchema"
p2:type="q5:string">Pride and Prejudice</Title>
        </q4:Book>
        <q6:Book id="id4" p2:type="q6:Book" xmlns:p2="http://www.
w3.org/2001/XMLSchema-instance" xmlns:q6="http://www.apress.com/Book">
                <Title xmlns:q7="http://www.w3.org/2001/XMLSchema"
p2:type="q7:string">To Kill a Mockingbird</Title>
        </q6:Book>
</Root>
```

We have everything that we had in our output before, but we also added, not just one, but three new elements. First, take a look at the Array element. Notice how there are now two Item elements as children of the Array. The second Item points to id4, which is our second book. The number of Item elements is directly proportional to the number of instances of SoapBook that are put in the List member of our SoapLibrary.

Deserializing

We have spent all our time so far with the serialization of XML, but we have not gotten to the deserialization. The deserialization of XML is quite easy and is just a single line. For the XML example below, we can just call the Deserialize method from the XmlSerializer instance.

```
<?xml version="1.0"?>
<Book xmlns:xsi="http://www.w3.org/2001/XMLSchema-instance"
xmlns:xsd="http://www.w3.org/2001/XMLSchema" Movie="false">
        <Title>Gone With the Wind</Title>Margaret Mitchell<Color>Two</Color>
</Book>
```

Using the following code, we are able to display the title of this book to our XML Viewer window, as shown in Figure 4-2.

```
Book book;
XmlSerializer serializer = new XmlSerializer(typeof(Book));
using (FileStream fs = new FileStream("book.xml",FileMode.Open))
{
    book = (Book)serializer.Deserialize(fs);
}
richTextBox1.AppendText(book.Title);
```

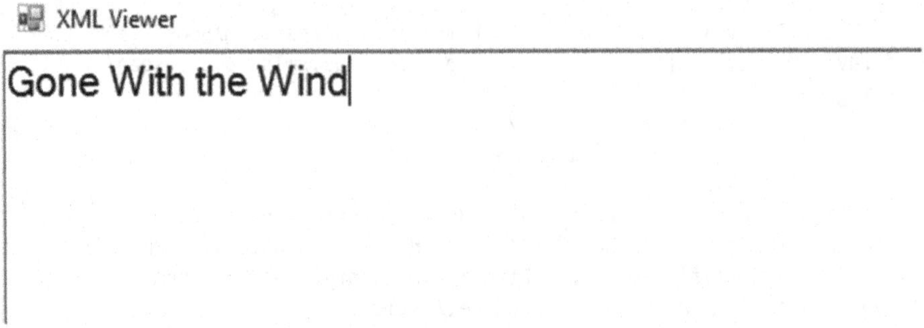

 XML Viewer

Gone With the Wind|

Figure 4-2. The output of the title from the book that was serialized

Just like serializing was difficult with the SOAP, we are going to have an even harder time deserializing our SOAP message. Luckily, we do not have to worry about that here as that would be handled by the Service Reference connection that would be handling the SOAP web calls. Because of that, we will avoid deserializing the SOAP XML manually since there will be more to it than just calling `Deserialize`. In fact, because we had to add the root element to the SOAP request, we would have to actually use either `XmlDocument` or `XDocument` to actually load the XML into memory and handle the deserialization manually.

CHAPTER 5

■ ■ ■

Real Life Examples

This chapter is all about putting the previous chapters into good use. There will be two smaller applications that will be written. First is going to be an application that will read a RSS feed and then turn that feed into a simple HTML table. The other example is going to build on what we have learned with the library XML examples by creating an XML-based library application.

RSS Feed Application

RSS, or Real Simple Syndication, is an XML-based format that allows people to know when something has been published or changed. This example will demonstrate how to use XmlDocument. The content creators will post to their RSS feed, which will allow the consumer to see when new content has been released. In our example, we will be connecting to the USAGov.edu's RSS feed.

We will start by creating a class called RssFeed. We add the following methods: GetItems, GetItemsByPartialTitle, GetItemsByTitle, GetUrl, GetItemByTitle, GetTitle, and then Save.

The GetItems and GetTitle are two simple methods that are just an XPath query to get all the items:

```
public XmlNodeList GetItems()
{
    return document.SelectNodes("rss/channel/item");
}
public string GetTitle(XmlNode item)
{
    XmlNode titleNode = item.SelectSingleNode("./title");
    if (titleNode == null) return string.Empty;
    return titleNode.InnerText;
}
```

Things get complicated when we want to get a partial item. For the methods that rely on a partial match, we dive into more complicated XPath. By using the contains() XPath expression, we are able to check to see if a specific node value contains the given value. This works in the same fashion that the Contains() method in C# does.

© Jonathan Hartwell 2017
J. Hartwell, *C# and XML Primer*, DOI 10.1007/978-1-4842-2595-0_5

```
public XmlNode GetItemByPartialTitle(string partialTitle)
{
    XmlNode titleNode = document.SelectSingleNode($"//item/title[contains(.
    ,\"{partialTitle}\")]/..");
    return titleNode;
}
public XmlNodeList GetItemsByPartialTitle(string partialTitle)
 {
    XmlNodeList titleElements = document.SelectNodes($"//item/title[contain
    s(.,\"{partialTitle}\")]/..");
    return titleElements;
 }
```

This method takes a string to match and then searches for a title that contains the value that is given. We then go up a level in order to get the item.

Finally, we have the Save method. This method contains more logic than one may think as the XmlDocument itself already has a Save method. The issue is, as we have seen previously, you are not able to directly copy a node from one XmlDocument to another. In order to copy the node, we need to create a separate XmlDocument and start by giving it a base root element structure with a string.

```
public void Save(string fileName)
{
  XmlDocument saveData = new XmlDocument();
  saveData.LoadXml("<rss></rss>");
  XmlNodeList nodes = document.SelectNodes("//item");

  foreach(XmlNode node in nodes)
  {
     XmlNode importedNode = saveData.ImportNode(node, true);
                    saveData.DocumentElement.AppendChild(importedNode);
  }
   saveData.Save(fileName);
}
```

This code will get us all we need from the RSS feed, but from there we need to transform the XML to HTML, which we will do with XSLT.

```
RssFeed feed = new RssFeed("https://www.usa.gov/rss/updates.xml");
XslCompiledTransform xslt = new XslCompiledTransform();
feed.Save("test.xml");
xslt.Load("RssFeedLink.xslt");
xslt.Transform("test.xml", "output.html");
```

The code for the XSLT transformation goes hand-in-hand with our ongoing example. We create a new XslCompileTransform, which will perform the transform in memory and then save it to a file, and then load the XSLT file, which will be shown later. We save our items from the RSS feed using our Save method on the feed instance of RssFeed and then call the Transform method. We pass the in and out paths and at the end we will get something that looks like the following:

Hurricane Matthew—Be Prepared http://connect.usa.gov/hurricane-matthew-be-prepared

Your Vote and the Electoral College https://www.usa.gov/features/your-vote-and-the-electoral-college

USAGov's 11 National Parks You Can't Miss in 2016 https://www.usa.gov/features/usagovs-11-national-parks-you-cant-miss-in-2016

Get Ready for School—8 Tips for Parents from Kids.gov https://www.usa.gov/features/get-ready-for-school-8-tips-for-parents-from-kids-gov

Figure 5-1.

The XSLT to create the transform not only uses a few basic XPath queries in order to get the information we want, but it also gives a basic idea of how to structure and write an XSLT file.

```
<?xml version="1.0" encoding="utf-8"?>
<xsl:stylesheet version="1.0" xmlns:xsl="http://www.w3.org/1999/XSL/
Transform"
    xmlns:msxsl="urn:schemas-microsoft-com:xslt" exclude-result-
prefixes="msxsl"
>
    <xsl:output method="html" indent="yes"/>

  <xsl:template match="/">
    <html>
      <xsl:apply-templates />
    </html>
  </xsl:template>

  <xsl:template match="item">
    <table>
      <td>
        <xsl:apply-templates select="./title"/>
      </td>
      <td>
        <xsl:apply-templates select="./link"/>
      </td>
    </table>
  </xsl:template>
  <xsl:template match="title">
    <xsl:value-of select="."/>
  </xsl:template>
  <xsl:template match="link">
    <xsl:variable name="url"><xsl:value-of select="." /></xsl:variable>
    <a href="{$url}"><xsl:value-of select="."/></a>
  </xsl:template>
</xsl:stylesheet>
```

There are four different templates. The first template, going from top to bottom, will match on the root element, which is "root" in our case. We call the apply-templates function on the root. What apply-templates does is iterate over the children of the parent node and then applies whichever template matches a specific element. In our case, it will match the item template because the only children of root are items. We create our table in the item template and then call two more templates: title and link. The title template will just extract the title from the title node using value-of. The link template is a bit more complicated as it uses variables in order to create valid HTML links. The reason why a variable must be used in this case is because the parser is not able to handle the way that the a anchor works in HTML combined with the XML. In order to get the value of the link, you must use the value-of function. This becomes a problem since that would put fully formed XML inside the text of the anchor tag, which causes malformed XML.

Following is the full code example:

The RssFeed Class

```
using System;
using System.Xml;

namespace RssFeedConverter
{
    public class RssFeed
    {
        public string Path { get; set; }
        private XmlDocument document;
        public RssFeed(string path)
        {
            Path = path;
            document = new XmlDocument();
            document.Load(Path);
        }

        /// <summary>
        /// Save the document
        /// </summary>
        public void Save(string fileName)
        {
            XmlDocument saveData = new XmlDocument();
            saveData.LoadXml("<rss></rss>");
            XmlNodeList nodes = document.SelectNodes("//item");

            foreach(XmlNode node in nodes)
            {
                XmlNode importedNode = saveData.ImportNode(node, true);
                saveData.DocumentElement.AppendChild(importedNode);
            }
            saveData.Save(fileName);
        }
    }
```

```csharp
/// <summary>
/// Get All Items from the feed
/// </summary>
/// <returns></returns>
public XmlNodeList GetItems()
{
    return document.SelectNodes("rss/channel/item");
}

public XmlNodeList GetItemsByPartialTitle(string partialTitle)
{
    XmlNodeList titleElements = document.SelectNodes($"//item/title[
    contains(.,\"{partialTitle}\")]/..");
    return titleElements;
}

public XmlNode GetItemByPartialTitle(string partialTitle)
{
    XmlNode titleNode = document.SelectSingleNode($"//item/title[con
    tains(.,\"{partialTitle}\")]/..");
    return titleNode;
}

public Uri GetUrl(XmlNode item)
{
    XmlNode urlNode = item.SelectSingleNode("./link");
    return new Uri(urlNode.InnerText);
}
/// <summary>
/// Get an item by a title
/// </summary>
/// <param name="title"></param>
/// <returns></returns>
public XmlNode GetItemByTitle(string title)
{
    XmlNode titleElement = document.SelectSingleNode($"//
    item[title=\"{title}\"]");
    if(titleElement.HasChildNodes)
    {
        XmlNode titleChild = titleElement.FirstChild;
        return titleChild;
    }
    return titleElement;
}

/// <summary>
/// Get the title from a
/// </summary>
```

```csharp
        public string GetTitle(XmlNode item)
        {
            XmlNode titleNode = item.SelectSingleNode("./title");
            if (titleNode == null) return string.Empty;
            return titleNode.InnerText;
        }
    }
}
```

Program.cs: Where the Code Is Run

```csharp
using System.Xml.Xsl;
namespace RssFeedConverter
{
    class Program
    {
        static void Main(string[] args)
        {
            RssFeed feed = new RssFeed("https://www.usa.gov/rss/updates.
xml");
            XslCompiledTransform xslt = new XslCompiledTransform();
            feed.Save("test.xml");
            xslt.Load("RssFeedLink.xslt");
            xslt.Transform("test.xml", "output.html");
        }
    }
}
```

The RssFeedLink XSLT Stylesheet

```xml
<?xml version="1.0" encoding="utf-8"?>
<xsl:stylesheet version="1.0" xmlns:xsl="http://www.w3.org/1999/XSL/
Transform"
    xmlns:msxsl="urn:schemas-microsoft-com:xslt" exclude-result-
prefixes="msxsl"
>
    <xsl:output method="html" indent="yes"/>

  <xsl:template match="/">
    <html>
      <xsl:apply-templates />
    </html>
  </xsl:template>

  <xsl:template match="item">
    <table>
      <td>
        <xsl:apply-templates select="./title"/>
```

```
      </td>
      <td>
        <xsl:apply-templates select="./link"/>
      </td>
    </table>
  </xsl:template>
  <xsl:template match="title">
    <xsl:value-of select="."/>
  </xsl:template>
  <xsl:template match="link">
    <xsl:variable name="url"><xsl:value-of select="." /></xsl:variable>
    <a href="{$url}"><xsl:value-of select="."/></a>
  </xsl:template>
</xsl:stylesheet>
```

Weather Application

Now let's take a look at a complex weather example for the forecast of a specific location. We will use LINQ to XML in order to get at the information we need. For this example, we want to get the seven-day forecast for high and lows. The XML file that is used in this example is large so it will be a separate file that will be on the web site. However, the code we need is rather short for the task that we want to execute.

```
using System.Collections.Generic;
using System.Linq;
using System.Xml.Linq;

namespace Weather
{
    class Program
    {
        static void Main(string[] args)
        {
            // Load the weather file
            XDocument document = XDocument.Load("weather.xml");

            // create the points that will be used later
            IEnumerable<Point> locations = document.Descendants("location")
                .Select(x => new Point()
                {
                    Key = x.Element("location-key").Value,
                    Lat = float.Parse(x.Element("point").
                    Attribute("latitude").Value),
                    Long = float.Parse(x.Element("point").
                    Attribute("longitude").Value)
                });
```

```
            List<Point> processedPoints = new List<Point>();
            // process each point
            foreach(Point p in locations)
            {
                // filter down to the necessary nodes
                XElement parameters = document.Descendants("parameters")
                                    .Where(x => x.Attribute("applicable-
                                    location").Value == p.Key).First();
                XElement maximimums = parameters.Descendants("temperature")
                                    .Where(x => x.Attribute("type").
Value == "maximum" && x.Name == "temperature").First();
                XElement minimums = parameters.Descendants("temperature")
                                    .Where(x => x.Attribute("type").Value ==
"minimum" && x.Name == "temperature").First();

                // iterate over all the elements in the maximum temperature
                element
                foreach(XElement max in maximimums.Descendants("value"))
                {
                    p.Highs.Add(int.Parse(max.Value));
                }

                // iterate over all the elements in the minimum temperature
                element
                // there can be an empty value element so have to take that
                into account
                foreach (XElement low in minimums.Descendants("value"))
                {
                    if (string.IsNullOrEmpty(low.Value)) continue;
                    p.Lows.Add(int.Parse(low.Value));
                }
                processedPoints.Add(p);
            }

            // Create a root element called temps
            XElement root = new XElement("temps");

            foreach(Point p in processedPoints)
            {
                // create a base element for each key and make the lat/long
                children
                // of the key element
                XElement element = new XElement(
                    p.Key,
                        new XElement("lat", p.Lat),
                        new XElement("long", p.Long)
                    );
                // create a new temperature element
```

```
            XElement temperature = new XElement("temperature");
            XElement highs = new XElement("high");
            foreach(int high in p.Highs)
            {
                XElement highElement = new XElement("value", high);
                highs.Add(highElement);
            }
            XElement lows = new XElement("lows");
            foreach(int low in p.Lows)
            {
                XElement lowElement = new XElement("value", low);
                lows.Add(lowElement);
            }
            temperature.Add(highs);
            temperature.Add(lows);
            element.Add(highs);
            element.Add(lows);
            root.Add(element);
        root.Add(temperature);
          }
        XDocument nw = new XDocument(root);
        nw.Save("temp.xml");
    }
}
public class Point
{
    public float Lat { get; set; }
    public float Long { get; set; }
    public string Key { get; set; }

    public Point()
    {
        Highs = new List<int>();
        Lows = new List<int>();
    }
    public List<int> Highs { get; set; }
    public List<int> Lows { get; set; }
}
}
```

The above code does all the work and it clocks in at 102 lines. We use LINQ to shorten the amount of code necessary in order to get at the elements that we want. Let's walk through what this application is doing.

A class named Point is created that stores the key global position in the form of latitude and longitude as well as all the highs and lows for the next seven days. We use the Descendents method in order to get all of the location elements in the XML document. We are able to create a Point instance for each location by using the Select LINQ extension and creating a Point. Once we have the Points, we can start processing on the XML document in order to find more information regarding these locations.

There is a filter to get the parameter elements from the document, which is where the temperature information is stored, and to find the specific element where the application-location attribute location is equal to the key that we stored in the previous section of code. We then use the parameters element to filter down even further to minimums and maximums. It is a good idea that we stored the parameter element because it means that we don't have to query the document again, which can cause performance issues with significanlty large XML files. We then iterate over the low and the high values for each and store them in a new processed point.

The most complex part comes in the form of creating a new document. It is relatively easy to create XML documents in LINQ to XML, but it can get unruly if you aren't careful in organizing the way that the code is written. We create several root elements, the base root which is called temps and then root elements for each other aspect of the XML we are saving. We then will add each root to the parent root until we get all the way up to the temps element. Once we get to that element, we know that the document is all ready and completed, so we can instantiate a new XDocment class with the instance of XElement we have called "root". After a call to Save on the XDocument instance, we have finished processing the XML document and receive the following output:

```xml
<?xml version="1.0" encoding="utf-8"?>
<temps>
  <point1>
    <lat>38.99</lat>
    <long>-77.02</long>
    <high>
      <value>72</value>
      <value>79</value>
      <value>82</value>
      <value>82</value>
      <value>76</value>
      <value>65</value>
      <value>65</value>
    </high>
    <lows>
      <value>58</value>
      <value>61</value>
      <value>63</value>
      <value>62</value>
      <value>59</value>
      <value>55</value>
    </lows>
  </point1>
  <point2>
    <lat>39.7</lat>
    <long>-104.8</long>
    <high>
      <value>85</value>
      <value>78</value>
      <value>65</value>
```

```
      <value>54</value>
      <value>54</value>
      <value>63</value>
      <value>68</value>
    </high>
    <lows>
      <value>50</value>
      <value>53</value>
      <value>44</value>
      <value>40</value>
      <value>34</value>
      <value>35</value>
      <value>40</value>
    </lows>
  </point2>
  <point3>
    <lat>47.6</lat>
    <long>-122.3</long>
    <high>
      <value>59</value>
      <value>58</value>
      <value>57</value>
      <value>58</value>
      <value>60</value>
      <value>58</value>
      <value>57</value>
    </high>
    <lows>
      <value>50</value>
      <value>49</value>
      <value>47</value>
      <value>48</value>
      <value>52</value>
      <value>49</value>
    </lows>
  </point3>
</temps>
```

A Basic XML Serializer

In Chapter 4 we went over the serialization of XML, but now we are going to use LINQ to XML to create our own basic serializer. This is going to be a naïve implementation that will be limited in what it will actually handle. For this application, we will be able to handle a single class that can allow for attributes as well as ignore properties. We will also be able to serialize and deserialize using streams.

The first thing that we need to do is create the attributes that we will use to indicate what needs to be serialized. For this we will create three attributes: Serializable, Ignore, and XmlAttribute. The Serializable attribute will be used solely on classes to determine if they are eligible for serialization. The Ignore attribute is an attribute that can only be used on properties. This attribute will suppress any property that is decorated with that property and will not serialize that property. Finally, the XmlAttribute attribute is going to be used to add an attribute to the property. Let's get started by declaring the attributes:

```
[AttributeUsage(AttributeTargets.Class)]
public class SerializableAttribute : Attribute
{
}
```

This attribute declaration is short, but it does a lot just because it is an attribute. First, we use an attribute that is built into .NET called AttributeUsage. This attribute helps limit the usage of the attribute. We only want the Serializable attribute on classes as it is not possible to just serialize a single property. This attribute is now ready to be used on any class.

Moving on to the XmlAttribute attribute, we need to add a bit more code in order to accomplish what we want:

```
[AttributeUsage(AttributeTargets.Property)]
public class XmlAttribute : Attribute
{
    public string Name { get; set; }
    public string Value { get; set; }
    public XmlAttribute(string name, object value)
    {
        if (value != null)
        {
            Value = value.ToString();
        }
        else
        {
            Value = string.Empty;
        }
        Name = name;
    }
}
```

Again we need to declare the AttributeUsage, but this time we only want to target properties. If we wanted to, we could allow this attribute to be usable on classes, but for this example we are just going to keep it on properties. One difference between this attribute and the SerializableAttribute is that XmlAttribute is using a constructor that takes two arguments. We do this so we can save the name of the attribute as well as the value of the attribute.

Our last attribute that we need to define is the ignore attribute that is aptly named IgnoreAttibute. This attribute is similar to the SerializableAttribute in that there is no real substance to the class.

```
[AttributeUsage(AttributeTargets.Property)]
public class IgnoreAttribute : Attribute
{
}
```

The only difference between the IgnoreAttribute and the SerializableAttribute is the AttributeUsage. It only makes sense that we want to decorate properties since, if we wanted to ignore a class, we just wouldn't use the SerializableAttribute.

Now that we have the attributes that we are going to use, we need to start implementing our serializer. There are two major functions we need this class to do: serialize and deserialize. Under the hood, we are going to use LINQ to XML in order to handle the backend XML. We can declare the shell of this class below:

```
public class XmlSerializer<T>
{
    private Type type;
    private string defaultNamespace;
    public XmlSerializer(string defaultNamespace)
    {
        type = typeof(T);
        this.defaultNamespace = defaultNamespace;
    }

    public T Deserialize(string filePath)
    {
    }

    public void Serialize(Stream stream, T serializableObject)
    {
    }

}
```

We have two private members, type and defaultNamespace. We want to save the type of the model that we are going to serialize as well as save a default namespace. We also make this a generic class, which saves a lot of typing for those who use this class as there is no need to pass in types in every method. However, the downside is that an XmlSerializer is tied to a single model type. Our Serialize method takes in a stream as well as the object of type T, which is the model that is going to be serialized.

Let's start implementing the methods on the XmlSerializer class. We will start by implementing the Serialize method:

```
public void Serialize(Stream stream, T serializableObject)
{
    // get the type of the passed in class
    Type type = typeof(T);
    // Check to see if the class has the Serializable attribute

    if(type.CustomAttributes.Any(x => x.AttributeType == typeof(Serializabl
    eAttribute)))
```

```
    {
        XElement element = new XElement(type.Name);
        // This class has the ability to be serialized since the
        serializable attribute was on the class
        PropertyInfo[] properties = type.GetProperties();
        // filter out properties that have the ignore on them
        List<PropertyInfo> serializableProperties = properties.Where(x => x.
        GetCustomAttribute(typeof(IgnoreAttribute)) == null).ToList();
        foreach (PropertyInfo pi in serializableProperties)
        {

            element.Add(CreateElement(pi, serializableObject));
        }
        byte[] bytes = Encoding.UTF8.GetBytes(element.ToString());
        stream.Write(bytes, 0, bytes.Length);
    }
}

private XElement CreateElement(PropertyInfo propertyInfo, T
serializableObject)
{
    XElement element = new XElement(propertyInfo.Name);
    XmlAttribute xmlAttribute = propertyInfo.GetCustomAttribute(typeof(XmlAt
    tribute)) as XmlAttribute;
    if (xmlAttribute != null)
    {
        element.Add(new XAttribute(xmlAttribute.Name, xmlAttribute.Value));
    }

        // create a child element using the property name and get the
        property value off of the passed in object
        element.Add(new XElement(propertyInfo.Name, type.
        GetProperty(propertyInfo.Name).GetValue(serializableObject, null).
        ToString()));

    return element;
}
```

We start by instantiating a Type class that is based on the type of the generic parameter. That type is going to be the type of the class that may need to be serialized. Since the SerializeAttribute is not mandatory, we do need to verify the class has that attribute before continuing. We do that by using the Any method that is a LINQ extension.

```
type.CustomAttributes.Any(x => x.AttributeType ==
typeof(SerializableAttribute))
```

We need to look through all of the custom attributes in order to check to see if this class is indeed decorated by SerializableAttribute. We do that by using the Any LINQ extension method that will iterated on the CustomAttributes collection and check to see if any of the attribute types are of type `SerializableAttribute`. Once it finds a single match, it will stop and return `true`.

Once we verify that this class is decorated by `SerializeAttribute`, we can start creating our XML. We start by creating an element that is given the same name as the serialized class. Next, we need to get all of the properties of this class. We can do that by using the `GetProperties` method on the `Type` instance. We then need to perform another check, which is to see if any of the properties are decorated with the `IgnoreAttribute`. After all, we want to ensure that our attributes behave in the expected manner. We filter the attributes using the Where LINQ extension method.

```
List<PropertyInfo> serializableProperties = properties.Where(x => x.GetCusto
mAttribute(typeof(IgnoreAttribute)) == null).ToList();
```

We are able to pull all of the properties that do not have the `IgnoreAttribute` decoration.

Now that we have the properties, we need to turn those into XML. We have the `PropertyInfo` instances that contain all of the information for each property on the class type of our model. In order to make the code more readable, we should break out the generation of the XML from a `PropertyInfo` instance into a separate private method. Our private method is named `CreateElement` because all it does is create new elements.

```
private XElement CreateElement(PropertyInfo propertyInfo, T
serializableObject)
{
    XElement element = new XElement(propertyInfo.Name);
    XmlAttribute xmlAttribute = propertyInfo.GetCustomAttribute(typeof
    (XmlAttribute)) as XmlAttribute;
    if (xmlAttribute != null)
    {
        element.Add(new XAttribute(xmlAttribute.Name, xmlAttribute.Value));
    }

        element.Add(new XElement(propertyInfo.Name, type.
GetProperty(propertyInfo.Name).GetValue(serializableObject, null).
ToString()));

    return element;
}
```

We start by instantiating a new instance of XElement and we give the name of that element the name of the property that is stored in the `PropertyInfo` instance. We then need to check to see if we need an attribute to this element by checking to see if the instance of `PropertyInfo` has the custom attribute `XmlAttribute`. We don't need to iterate over anything because we already have a single instance of `PropertyInfo` so, instead of iteration, we can just call the `GetCustomAttribute` method, which takes in a type and returns an instance of `System.Attribute`. Since we know what we should be getting in return, we can see if we can cast to an `XmlAttribute` instance. This attribute may not exist on a property, so we need to do a null check to make sure that we are only adding attributes to properties that have them declared. If we do find an XmlAttribute decoration on this property, we then go ahead and add an XAttribute instance to our current XElement instance, which contains the property we are currently inspecting. We then go ahead and create a child XElement that contains the property name as well as the value of the property, converted to string. Remember XML does not have datatypes so we need to ensure that everything we add to the XML is in a string form.

Finally, we can convert our XML into a byte array so that we can serialize to the stream that was passed in:

```
byte[] bytes = Encoding.UTF8.GetBytes(element.ToString());
stream.Write(bytes, 0, bytes.Length);
```

We need to convert our XML element into a byte array so we use the Encoding class that is the System.Text namespace. There are many different encodings that we can use, but seeing as C# has UTF-8 strings, it would make sense to encode our XML as UTF-8 instead of ANSI. Now we have a byte array that we can write to our stream. Once the XML is written to the stream, the Serialize method is done with its processing and gives control back to the calling method.

Our Deserialize method is much shorter than our Serialize method, but it is a more complicated method that dives into reflection quite a bit:

```
public T Deserialize(string filePath)
{
    T loaded = Activator.CreateInstance<T>();
    XDocument doc = XDocument.Load(filePath);
    XElement root = doc.Root;
    if (root.Name == typeof(T).Name)
    {
        foreach(XElement child in root.Elements())
        {
            /// Check to see if this is a class or just a property

                loaded.GetType().GetProperty(child.Name.ToString()).
                SetValue(loaded, child.Value);

        }
    }
    else
    {
        throw new ArgumentException("The type passed in does not match the
        XML");
    }
    return loaded;
}
```

In order to add data to any class, we need an instance of that class. The Activator class has a method called CreateInstance, which does what the name says and creates an instance of the type passed in. We need this instance; otherwise, there would be no state persisted.

Now that we have an instance that we can save data to, we need to load our XML from the file that is passed in. We declare a new XDocument and load the XML as we have done before in Chapter 2. We need to get the root element so we have something to start with. Because we are deserializing this XML into a C# class, we need to ensure that the class that is passed in through the generic parameter is the same name as the root element name. If it is not the same, then we throw an exception and stop processing; otherwise, we need to continue deserialization. We then iterate over the elements of the root element and make the same checks as we did with the class to ensure that the names match, but this time we look at properties instead of class name. Notice that we are using Elements() method instead of Descendants(). We do this because we only want to go one level deeper, getting only the children of the current element while not touching the grandchildren. Since we are using properties, it does not matter if there are properties missing from the XML as it will not affect properties that aren't instantiated properties from the load. If you are using reference types as properties on your class, you must make sure to instantiate them in the constructor. Otherwise, you risk getting a NullReferenceException.

Now comes the magic of reflection. We have the default instance of our model class, but we need to add data to those properties. However, we aren't able to directly call those properties to modify them, so we need to pull some reflection tricks out of our sleeves. We need to first get the type of our default instance of our model class using the GetType() method. We then need to get the property that we are looking to modify by using the GetProperty method. This method takes a string as its argument and looks up the property based on that string. Luckily, we already know the property name since it is the name of the element we are currently looking at. We now have the PropertyInfo for the property we want to modify, so we then need to call the SetValue method. This method takes two arguments: the source object and the value to set. The source object in this case is the default instance of our model class. We then set that value to the string of the element value. As I noted before, this is a naïve and simple example, which means we are not accounting for cases such as non-string properties or nested XML. Once we populate the data, the only thing left to do is to return the instance of the model class.

We have the serialization and deserialization coded and ready to go, so now we just need a model class. Lets create a book class and give it a few properties:

```
[Serializable]
public class Book
{
    [XmlAttribute("Notes","The first book of seven")]
    public string Title { get; set; }
    public string Author { get; set; }
    public string Year { get; set; }
}
```

We are using two of the three custom attributes in this model: SerializableAttribute and XmlAttribute. We have three properties: title, author, and year. We want to have an attribute on the Title element, which we are calling notes. When we run the serializer method from the XmlSerializer instance, we get the following output:

```
<Book>
  <Title Notes="The first book of seven">
    <Title>Harry Potter and the Sorcerer's Stone</Title>
  </Title>
  432799_1_En
    432799_1_EnJK Rowling</Author>
  </Author>
  <Year>
    <Year>1997</Year>
  </Year>
</Book>
```

It shouldn't be a surpise what the output is as it should be expect based on the Book class model. However, what if we want to hide the year property on this book? We can do that by just using the IgnoreAttrbute. Our new Book class becomes the following:

```
[Serializable]
public class Book
{
    [XmlAttribute("Notes","The first book of seven")]
    public string Title { get; set; }
    public string Author { get; set; }
    [Ignore]
    public string Year { get; set; }
}
```

This yields the following XML:

```
<Book>
  <Title Notes="The first book of seven">
    <Title>Harry Potter and the Sorcerer's Stone</Title>
  </Title>
  432799_1_En
    432799_1_EnJK Rowling</Author>
  </Author>
</Book>
```

With some reflection tricks as well as using LINQ to XML, we have demostrated a simple way that the serialization of XML in .NET works. Now there are always ways to improve this code such as handling nested elements (for instance, creating a Library class that has multiple Book classes as properties). We could also add better exception handling as well, but I believe that this example can give a better understanding of what is happening under the hood and how the methods we learned before can be used as a base level to build upon.

Index

A, B

AppendChild method, 28–29
Attribute method, 26

C

CreateAttribute method, 26
CreateElement method, 27–28
CreateInstance, 83

D

Descendants(), 83

E

Element method, 20
Elements() method, 83
Extensible Markup Language (XML)
    attributes, 11–13, 19
        adding, 26–27
        modifying, 24–25
        removing, 32–33
    Document *vs.* Document.Root, 19
    elements, 1–2
        adding, 27–30
        modifying, 25–26
        removing, 33–34
    handling namespaces, 13–14
    library.xml, 7–8
    LINQ, 18
        adding attributes, 38–39
        adding elements, 39–40
        merging documents, 40–42
        modifying attributes, 35–37
        modifying elements, 37–38
        removing attributes, 42–43
        removing elements, 43
        saving, 44
    loading, 8
    merging documents, 30–32
    saving, 34–35
    transforming results, 20
    using XPath with
        XDocument, 21
    XmlDocument/
        XDocument, 23–24
    XmlReader, 15–17
    XPath, 2–3, 8–11
    XPathDocument, 15
    XSLT, 3–4
Extensible Stylesheet Language
    (XSLT), 3–4

F

FileStream, 46
Flush method, 46

G, H

GetCustomAttribute method, 81
GetProperties method, 81, 83

I, J, K, L, M

IgnoreAttrbute, 84
ImportNode method, 31
Inheritance, 55–57
InnerText property, 25

© Jonathan Hartwell 2017
J. Hartwell, *C# and XML Primer*, DOI 10.1007/978-1-4842-2595-0

Get the eBook for only $4.99!

Why limit yourself?

Now you can take the weightless companion with you wherever you go and access your content on your PC, phone, tablet, or reader.

Since you've purchased this print book, we are happy to offer you the eBook for just $4.99.

Convenient and fully searchable, the PDF version enables you to easily find and copy code—or perform examples by quickly toggling between instructions and applications.

To learn more, go to http://www.apress.com/us/shop/companion or contact support@apress.com.

Printed in the United States
By Bookmasters